2003-04

FIGHTING ILLINI

BASKETBALL

FAN GUIDE

OFFICIALLY LICENSED BY THE
UNIVERSITY OF ILLINOIS

ILLINOIS

SPORTS
PUBLISHING
L.L.C.

www.SportsPublishingLLC.com

Executive Editor: **Kent Brown**
Editorial Assistance: **Derrick Burson, Travis Steiner, Michelle Warner**
Photography (unless otherwise noted): **Mark Jones, Mark Cowan, Dan Donovan, Glenn James, Tom Schaefges, Sharon Walker, Steve Woltmann**

Publisher: **Peter L. Bannon**

Senior Managing Editor: **Susan M. Moyer**

Developmental Editor: **Doug Hoepker**

Copy Editor: **Holly Birch**

Art Director: **K. Jeffrey Higgerson**

Cover Design: **Joseph Brumleve**

Book Layout:
Kerri Baker, Tracy Gaudreau, Greg Hickman, Jennifer L. Polson

Imaging: **Kenneth J. O'Brien**

Front Cover Photo: **Jonathan Daniel/Getty Images**

ISBN: 1-58261-013-4

Yours Are The Hands That Hold Us

HIGH

The University of Illinois is one of the finest institutions in the country, enabling the most talented and dedicated student-athletes to participate in collegiate athletics. The success started long ago and that long-standing tradition carries us into a bright future.

Within the I FUND, our supporters are given the opportunity to change lives one student-athlete at a time. With your contributions, we can continue to provide the most experienced coaches, spirited administrators and determined academic support staff to guide our student-athletes to success on and off the playing field.

Be "the hands that hold us high" by becoming involved in a student-athlete's future and the future successes of our Illini Family.

THE I FUND
Investing in a Brilliant Future

1700 S. Fourth Street
Champaign, IL
217/333-6277

Shawn Wax, Director of Development
wax@uiuc.edu
Ken Zimmerman, Director of Major Gifts
kzimmerm@uiuc.edu
Mike Hatfield, Associate Director
mhatfiel@uiuc.edu
Carrie Wilson, Assistant Director
cewilso@uiuc.edu

Illini Center, 200 S. Wacker Drive
Chicago, IL
312/575-7850

Steve Greene,
Director of Development I FUND Chicago
jsgreene@uiuc.edu
Chris Tuttle,
Assistant Director, I FUND Chicago
Director, Varsity I Association
c-tuttle@uiuc.edu

Table of Contents

Where Have You Gone, Kevin Turner? 7

A Summer to Remember: Brian Cook Heads Way Out West 8

New Man on Campus: Introducing Coach Weber 14

Where Have You Gone, Bruce Douglas? 19

An Off-season Rollercoaster Ride 21

2003-04 Fighting Illini Season Preview 28

Where Have You Gone, Jerry Hester? 34

2003-04 Fighting Illini Roster 35

Meet the Fighting Illini: Player Profiles 36

Fighting Illini Coaching Staff 56

Where Have You Gone, Kenny Battle? 62

Illini Sports Network 63

2003-04 Fighting Illini Season Schedule 64

Opponent Profiles 66

Where Have You Gone, Victor Chukwudebe? 87

Big Ten Composite Schedule 88

2002-03 Fighting Illini Season in Review 90

Where Have You Gone, Richard Keene? 96

Where Have You Gone, Kevin Turner?

Kevin Turner played two years for both Lou Henson and Lon Kruger at UI. The Chicago native was a good example of hard work paying off. After averaging 10 points per game as a junior, number 33 closed out his career with a team-best 17 points per game on the way to a Big Ten title his senior year.

What are you doing these days?

I've been playing in Poland for the last five years, but I hope to play in the CBA this year. The season starts next month. Poland's been a great experience—traveling, learning new cultures, meeting guys. Last season, Damir [Krupalija] played in the same league as me.

Can you make a good living playing in Europe?

Yes. You can make $70,000 to $80,000 all the way up to $300,000 to $400,000. It's all about being on a good team. I want to play in the CBA (this year), because it gives you exposure for a possible call-up to the NBA. I want to give it one more shot before I get too old. If I can't make it here, I'll go back overseas.

What's your greatest memory of your time spent at UI?

My senior year was a break-out season for me and we won the Big Ten. That's something that's going to stick with me forever. I still wear that ring and the old '98 t-shirt with holes in it. I've washed it so many times. It's been overseas and everything.

Which of your former teammates do you stay in touch with?

Most of them. Jerry Gee and I still work out together. Jerry Hester. Kiwane [Garris]. I haven't seen Shelly Clark in a long time and then I saw him this morning. Bryant Notree plays overseas too. We're still close. Hester, Gee,

and I were in Poland together for three years in the same league.

What's the most significant thing that has happened for you since you left UI?

Just having the opportunity to go overseas. Not many people from where I'm from have been there. I love it there. I even thought about living there all year long, forever.

What do you miss most about Champaign-Urbana?

I miss the college life. Jerry Gee and I were just talking about it last week. Class, practice, going to the bars, girls, all those things. The real world's a lot different. You have obligations and have to depend on yourself.

Who's your favorite current Illini?

I like a lot of guys on the team. I know Jerrance. He's a good person. Dee's a tough kid. I know Luther—he's a good kid. I really like Roger Powell 'cause he's one of the underrated guys. He had some good games last year. Reminds me of myself early in my career. I mostly keep up with them on the internet. It became one of my hobbies. That was a cheaper way to keep in contact with people back home. The only college games we could watch [in Poland] were the Final Four. That's it. No ESPN in Poland. They have Eurosport, an equivalent, but no ESPN. I even started liking soccer.

Have you met Coach Weber?

No. I know he had some good seasons at Southern though. I heard he was an assistant at Purdue. I wish him a lot of luck.

A Summer to Remember
Brian Cook Heads Way Out West

By Mark Tupper

The Cook Company—Brian and mother Joyce—have always gotten by on whatever they could scrape together.

When times were tough growing up in Lincoln, Illinois, Brian Cook and his mother shared scraps of food, relied on relatives to help with an occasional meal or piece of clothing and always leaned on the one and only thing they knew they could depend on—each other.

"Money was something we didn't always have much of," Cook said, looking back matter-of-factly.

But the fortunes of Cook Co. began to change significantly this summer after Brian was drafted by the Los Angeles Lakers in the first round of the National Basketball Association draft. When his name was called on June 26—kicking off a celebration that tipped Lincoln on its ear—he became only the second University of Illinois player taken in the first round since Kendall Gill was picked by Charlotte in 1990. Frank Williams broke the long drought in 2002 when he went in the first round to the New York Knicks.

Sudden Fame, Same Smile

Suddenly, Brian Cook was a pro, a millionaire, a celebrity beyond anything he'd ever known and an instant member of one of sport's most compelling franchises.

Yes, it was a whirlwind summer for Brian Cook, who got a jump on things by finishing his four-year college career in grand style, winning the Big Ten Conference scoring title, the league's Player of the Year award, team MVP honors, and securing a permanent place in Illini lore by earning recognition as a committed student-athlete who consistently represented the university and Central Illinois in a first-rate manner.

That was a message Cook heard throughout the summer as well-wishers swarmed him with congratulations, best wishes and advice about his bright future.

"I'll tell you one thing," a woman said as she leaned in close to offer her piece of advice to Cook this summer.

"I only want to read about you on the sports page."

She smiled and patted Cook's hand and he nodded in understanding. Her reference, of course, was to Cook's new teammate—Kobe Bryant—who was Page One news after being charged in a sexual assault case.

"You won't have to worry about that," Cook answered politely.

Stepping toward his new white Cadillac Escalade, the first extravagance he allowed himself after signing a three-year deal with the Lakers, Cook admitted "[My life is] crazier than I ever imagined."

Goods On Display

Cook's post-Illini summer began when he and his mother teamed up to choose an agent, finally picking University of Illinois alum Mark Bartelstein of Chicago.

"He's the guy I felt most comfortable with," Cook said. "And that's going to be important to me."

Almost immediately, Bartelstein & Associates began handling Cook's ultra-busy calendar, a day planner filled with obligations. One of those obligations was to meet with NBA teams who wanted him to work out and interview with team officials. Cook jetted from one coast to the other and back again, working out individually against other prospects or in mock games. Whatever teams asked, Cook did.

"It was like a world tour," Cook said. "It seems I worked out for just about every team in the NBA. It isn't the workouts that wear you down. It's the flying around, going from plane to plane. That's the tiring part."

Finally, after one last workout for the New York Knicks, Cook flew home to be with his family and friends on an evening that would prove to test his nerves like no other—the night of the NBA draft.

Draft Night Jitters

Joyce Cook arranged to hold the draft party at the American Legion Post 263 in Lincoln, and on June 26 relatives, former classmates and teammates, teachers,

coaches, friends and media representatives packed in around a big-screen TV to wait for a familiar name to be called.

"Man, I'm nervous," Cook said at the beginning of the night. "I feel like I might throw up."

It was an agonizing evening as Cook sat nervously with his mother, girlfriend Melissa Williamson and a representative from Bartelstein's agency.

Behind them a throng of well-wishers shared in Brian's anxious wait as the first dozen picks were announced.

Then 15. Then 20. And still no team had selected Brian Cook, forward, University of Illinois.

Cook stirred, and for a moment you thought he really might throw up. The tension was immense.

And then, finally, with the 24th pick in the first round of the draft, the Los Angeles Lakers made their selection, and when the audio from the television leaked the single word, "Brian...," the American Legion hall erupted.

Brian and Joyce Cook hugged for a full 20 seconds. There were hugs and high-fives all around. Tears flowed throughout the room, starting with the moist traces that trickled down Brian Cook's cheeks.

"I feel great," he said. "It's been my dream to play in the NBA, and I feel it's a great situation for me. When the pick finally came, it was just a lot of emotion let off. I was waiting a long, long time and I was getting kind of nervous.

"My father played in the league. I was born with a ball in my crib. I made my first shot when I was three, and it's always been my dream."

One of those attending the draft party was former Illini assistant coach Rob Judson, who recruited Brian to play at Illinois, and who now heads the basketball program at Northern Illinois University.

"I really wanted him to go to the Western Conference, because I think the West suits his game more," Judson said. "Boy, the Lakers. Let's just hope Phil Jackson stays around a little bit, because Brian would be great in his triangle offense. He can shoot, come off screens and move.

"I'm happy for Brian and I'm happy for Joyce. She sacrificed a lot to get him this far."

No one was more pleased than Joyce Cook, even if it meant acknowledging a time when her son would be moving on.

"His dream finally came true," she said. "I wish he was a little closer, but that's OK. He made it. Proud is not a word I can use. I have no idea how you could explain it. Love. Proud. I have no idea. He's the greatest."

Brian Cook would soon find out most of Central Illinois felt the same way, but not before his life got even crazier.

Welcome to Tinsel Town

The day after the draft, Cook received a phone call from coach Phil Jackson, who welcomed him aboard. A couple days later he was jetting off to Los Angeles to meet with the L.A. media and club officials. After wearing jersey No. 34 at Illinois, he knew he'd have to make a change.

"Shaq has No. 34," Cook said of the Lakers' All-Star center. "I don't think I'd better ask him for it."

So, adding the "3" and the "4" together, Cook chose No. 7. Nevertheless, when he arrived in Los Angeles and was introduced along with fellow draft pick Luke Walton of Arizona, the team equipment manager hadn't come up with a No. 7 jersey. So Cook posed with No. 43, a number he'll never wear.

Cook made his professional debut in Long Beach, Calif., at the Summer Pro League, playing for former Lakers player Kurt Rambis. He made a strong showing, drawing positive reviews when he popped in 21 points and grabbed nine rebounds against the Los Angeles Clippers.

"The Summer Pro League was a good experience," he said after returning to Central Illinois. "I played pretty well. They were happy with the way I rebounded the ball. I committed too many fouls. Man, the game is really fast and physical. But that's OK. I'm learning."

Hometown Pride

Back home in Central Illinois, Cook was a bit stunned by how warmly he was received at a series of autograph sessions to correspond with the release of his book, *Brian Cook: An Illini Legend,* published by Sports Publishing L.L.C. of Champaign.

The first book signing took place in his hometown, and Lincoln turned out in big numbers, buying 800 copies of his book while posing for photographs and sharing stories, many of which began, "Remember when ..."

Subsequent book signings in Springfield, Mahomet, Champaign, Decatur and again in Lincoln drew long lines of well-wishers.

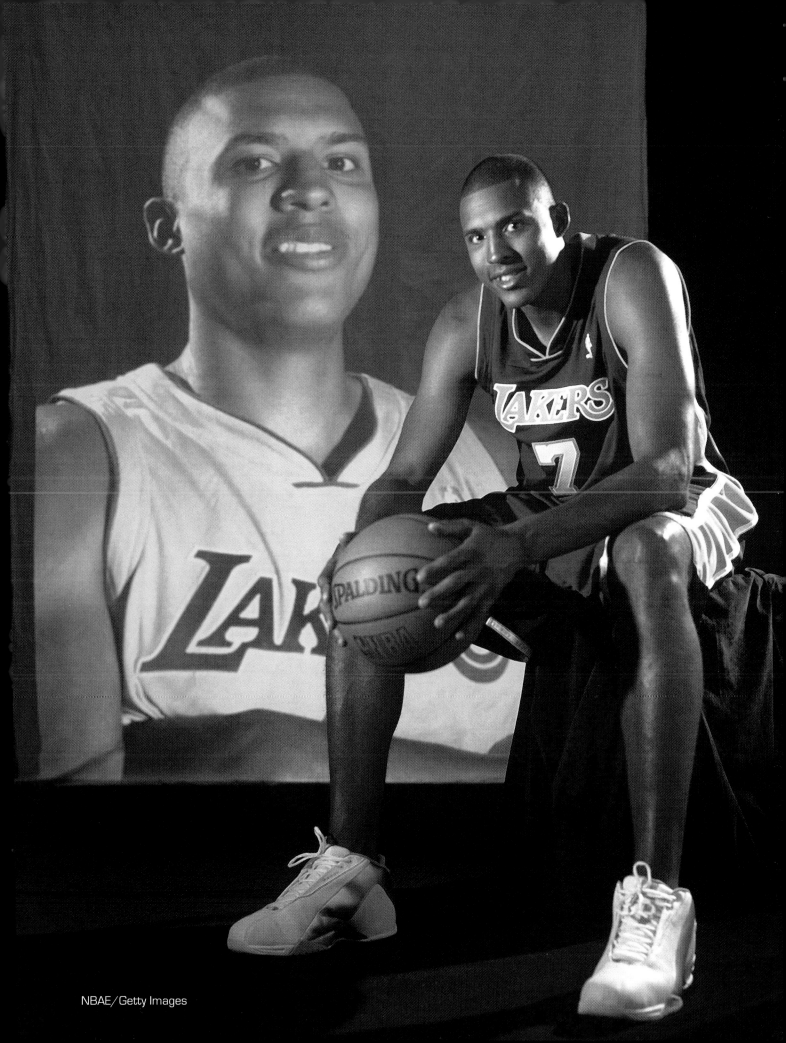

Cook slams it home against the Los Angeles Clippers during a game in June in the Southern California Summer League.

Many came so he could autograph the book. Some just wanted to tell him how much enjoyment he'd given them during his Illini career. Some handed over neatly arranged scrapbooks they'd compiled since the day he arrived in Champaign. And nearly all of them expressed sincere thank yous combined with best wishes on his new life.

"Do us proud," they typically said.

"It's amazing," Cook said. "You really don't realize you affect people like this. These people have been incredible."

When there was finally a break in the action, Cook rounded up a few of his long-time buddies and took them up to Minnesota so they could do what they like to do best—fish and enjoy their friendship.

He even found time to get back to campus and play a pickup game with his old Illini teammates, showing up at the Ubben Basketball Complex in time to give coach Bruce Weber a 10th player while Illinois was preparing for its exhibition tour overseas.

By the end of summer, word leaked that Brian and Melissa Williamson had become engaged, their marriage to happen sometime in the summer of 2004.

The couple picked out an apartment on the water in Marina del Rey, and Brian confessed that Melissa would be in charge of picking out the furniture.

"That's not my thing," he said.

Rules to Live By

Before departing for training camp, one final obligation remained. That was a trip to New York to participate in the NBA's rookie orientation session. With the Kobe Bryant situation still hot news, never has the NBA had a more relevant topic to show its newcomers.

Essentially, the rookies were told their lives had changed forever. They now reside in a storefront window on Main Street, where everyone in the world is watching their every move.

Invest your money intelligently. Beware of men and women who want that money and will do anything to get it. Handle your celebrity stature wisely and politely. In short: You've been handed the chance of a lifetime. Don't blow it.

It's a lesson Cook said he doesn't worry about, even though he's headed to one of the fastest moving cities in the world.

"You don't have to worry about that," he said. "I'm not a big party guy anyhow. I just want to find a lake when I have the time to fish."

On Sept. 28, Cook was off to Hawaii where the Lakers hold their training camp.

Phil Jackson said it's destined to be a most unusual season, with the arrival of newcomers Karl Malone and Gary Payton and the looming specter of Kobe Bryant's trial.

Typically, Cook is taking it all in stride.

"I don't care who they've brought in," he said. "I'm going to learn from all of them. I'm going to do what I did at Illinois—work hard and do the best I can.

"And as for Kobe, I still haven't met him. So I don't know any more about his deal than you do."

No, but Brian Cook is about to discover more about the Los Angeles Lakers than any of us will ever know, now that the former Illini great has become one.

YOU'VE TAKEN THE TEST DRIVE.
WE CAN FINANCE THE RIDE HOME.
WE LIVE WHERE YOU LIVE.™

For your next car loan, turn to the person who knows just how much your set of wheels means to you. Your State Farm agent. For information about car loans from *State Farm Bank®*, see your participating local State Farm agent, call 1-877-SF4-BANK or visit *statefarm.com*

LIKE A GOOD NEIGHBOR, STATE FARM IS THERE.®

New Man on Campus
Introducing Coach Weber

By Scott Musgrave

Bruce Weber won 103 games in his five seasons as men's basketball coach at Southern Illinois University, but it may have been one of his 54 losses that earned him the head coaching job at the University of Illinois.

On Nov. 21, 2002, Weber's Salukis lost a 75-72 decision to the Fighting Illini in the championship game of the Las Vegas Invitational. SIU led most of the second half, and as Weber says, "If we had scored one more basket, we win the game."

They didn't but the game made quite an impression with Ron Guenther. Just a year and a half later the UI athletic director hired Weber to replace the departed Bill Self.

Recently, I sat down to talk with Weber, the 16th coach in Illinois basketball history.

How has your new job at the University of Illinois measured up to your expectations?

I just think the attention has been overwhelming. The interest in Illinois basketball is just beyond any of my expectations. And I had been in the Big Ten before. I watched [Purdue] coach Gene Keady for 18 years, with good teams, and it's still way beyond what I ever thought. It makes your head spin a little. I mean, we had a recruit here over the weekend and he said, "You can run for governor and you haven't even won a game." It's good and bad. I think when you're not successful they're on your tail too.

When did you realize, "This isn't SIU anymore?"

That first morning I got here at 6:30 in the morning and just walked in the Ubben Complex. I had never been in this building. When I left Purdue they were just building it. And then to walk into the press conference was just beyond what I ever imagined it would be. When I did the press conference at Southern Illinois it was in a little classroom with 20 to 30 people. Here it was a big production. Just walking in this building that first morning, the office, everything, it's just on another level. Then walking out into the press conference was just special; you realize what level you're at and how important it is.

Don't pinch me yet?

Yeah. You look around and it's like, *wooo*…Hey, there's a little more pressure. This is important.

There's a saying, "Be careful what you wish for, you just might get it." Did that ever cross your mind?

Actually, a week before I got the job, it was crazy, I was with [Minnesota coach] Dan Monson watching a kid, and just kind of talking, more about Mark Few at Gonzaga. And Dan's gone through a lot there—probation and all that, guys leaving early, and he just said, "Hey, unless you really get [offered] something good, be happy at Southern Illinois." Then, when I got the job, all of a sudden, you get what you wish for.

Are you busier here than at SIU?

At Southern we washed practice jerseys. We had to fundraise. We did everything. So, in a way, there's a lot of things I don't have to do anymore. But, there are a lot of things that have taken their place.

More speaking engagements?

Yeah. My first one was a breakfast at Decatur on the second or third day after I got the job, and there were 700 people there. My first one at Southern I did one for four people. I did a lot [at Southern] for nine to 10 people. Like I said, there's just more attention paid to it here. Everything you say, people listen to. It was kind of a rude awakening I guess you'd say. I went to Taylorville [for an engagement], about an hour and forty-five minute drive I guess, and by the time I got back, the coaches already knew what I said because somebody had gone to the internet boards and posted everything.

What about your family? How are they adjusting?

It's hard when you move. I think it was really neat for them to be at the press conference. They got flown up on a nice plane and then the press conference was such a big-time thing. It was kind of overwhelming. Then, they go back to school and start thinking, "We're leaving our friends"—the reality check of that. Then we tried to bring them back a couple of times to get acclimated and meet some people. There were really three months, 90-something days in a hotel, that I was gone from them. But I think it was the best thing, because I could get so much more done here. Our whole staff did the same thing. No one brought their families. But it allowed my family to enjoy their summer and the transition. It's been good. When we moved to Carbondale I would say it took until that first Christmas to really settle in. For me, I think it'll be a full year before I settle in. Come see me next May, and I'll have a better grasp of it all.

Spare time is a rarity, but what do you like to do away from the job?

I walk every morning. My wife and I get the kids to school, then we walk. It's good exercise. Then we can talk, too. So, we walk the dogs and try to go a mile and a half to two miles. Then at night, after they've all gone to bed, I like to sit and have a beer and some popcorn and watch *SportsCenter*. For me that's like relaxing. I like the Packers. I've always been a Packers fan. I'll try to watch them. I like to watch Charles Barkley on TNT, if I don't have game film to watch. But that's kinda the relaxing thing I do.

Back to your hiring. When did you think you had a legitimate shot?

The first time I really even thought about it was on that Monday morning I was recruiting and I read the *St. Louis Post-Dispatch*, and it was Ron Guenther's quotes about what he was looking for. I told my assistant, "If he's telling the truth, I'm gonna get this job." And he just looked at me and laughed. But later on I found out Ron had me in mind, so some of the stuff he said related to me, I guess. Then, I thought I had a legit shot. I started getting calls from people he told not to call me. The funny one was Coach Keady. I just called him out of the blue about something else and he said something like, "Did you take it?" I was like, "What?" I really had no idea what he was talking about. I said, "Take what, Coach?" And he's like, "Don't give me that. Guenther's already called here three times in the last two days." Then he says, "Well if you're not gonna take it, tell me. I'll take it." I said, "Coach, I haven't talked to anyone." Then I had some calls from other guys, too. Then I got a call late in the week from Ron, and his thing was to keep it out of the papers. He said it was best for everyone and wanted to meet. Then I felt really good about it because I knew how he usually targeted one guy. But then I found out there were more people involved, so I had a little bit of doubt in my mind. I thought I was in good shape until Sunday night. I thought he'd call on Sunday night and he didn't. But he called the next morning at around 6:30. I think he wanted to sleep on it.

When you left Purdue did you think you'd someday go back and replace Gene Keady?

Getting a basketball job at a major school is so much about the timing. It's just the way the profession works. People hire people they're comfortable with—that they know. So, I thought logically, there were a lot of people that thought I'd end up at Purdue someday. But when this came up, my wife and I talked, and I talked with other people. I always think things happen for the best, and there's always a reason. Maybe I don't wanna be in Coach's shadow. We always felt it was a great job.

Coach Keady has a gruff persona, but what's he really like?

I always joke that he's really a big puppy dog. He's got that loud bark, but once you get to know him, he's really a good person. He's big-hearted. I think he's good-hearted. He's very funny, too.

What's the most important thing you learned from Coach Keady?

I think he's got to be one of the best motivators out there. He's very personable with the kids, and they react to him. The one thing I've learned is, no matter what happens, they're kids and you've got to help them. You've got to be there for them. Sometimes you're so mad at them. It's like the way things are with your own kids. They do stupid things. They make bad decisions, but you still have to help them.

Do you look forward to the two meetings with Purdue this season?

I'll be really excited, but once the ball goes up I don't even pay attention to who's on the other end. I coach. But after the game, if we beat him, I won't feel good about it. It's like beating your dad. You don't want to beat your dad.

Let's talk about your new team at the University of Illinois. How important was the trip to Europe this summer?

It was phenomenal. The first game we really struggled, but some of that was being so out of whack from travel. I actually liked when things went wrong because I could use them

Day one in his new office: Weber checks his watch between telephone interviews as player Jack Ingram waits for his turn with Coach.

as teaching points. Now they know how I feel about things instead of later in the season. From somebody being late for the bus, to staying out too late, not guarding somebody, not getting along, whatever, that trip was tremendous. I think after the first couple of games, as coaches we just said, "Man, this is so good." We're fast-forwarding. We're getting so much done. Now, they'll have a better feel. It was a tremendous, valuable thing. And it was a great experience for the kids. Those trips are one of the greatest things that happen in college sports. That opportunity to go and see another culture, things you'd never see, besides the bonding of the players. I know if you talk to our guys, those are things they'll remember for the rest of their lives.

What do you like most about the guys on your team?

They're good kids. And I didn't know that coming into this job. I had good kids at South-

ern, and that's why we won—because they listened. I mean, everyone has problems. It's not like I never had to discipline. I had to sit a guy at the NCAA tournament for being late. So, they're good kids. Obviously, we're very talented athletically. Now, my question is leadership, maturity on the court, a go-to guy on the court. And then, defending will be a big key they have to buy in on. We're so talented offensively, but if you're going to go on the road and win in the Big Ten, you've got to guard. And if you're going to go anywhere in the NCAA tournament, you've got to guard. And they've got to believe that. Until they believe it, we'll be good. But will we beat the really good teams? I think that'll be the question. And having a post guy is important. We lost Brian Cook. He carried them a lot last year. He came back and practiced with us because we didn't have enough people. We just looked at each other as a staff. I mean, *wooo*, this guy's good. He just dominated us. He was toying with us. You could tell he was a pro compared to everybody else. And we thought these guys we had were good.

Tell us about the new guys. Let's start with Richard McBride.

Richard is a good shooter. He's got a strong body but he's never lifted. He struggled in the weight room in the summer. It's just a natural body thing. His deal will be achieving success as a student-athlete. Freshmen that have success are ones that have the easiest transition in all phases. School isn't overwhelming. Social life is not overwhelming. Basketball is not overwhelming. If they can have an even keel, they usually have success. Basketball-wise, he needs to work on defense.

What about Brian Randle?

He's very talented athletically—naturally gifted. I think he has the best vertical jump on the team. He just kept going on the vertical jump test. He has to make the transition from being an inside guy to more of a perimeter guy—a swingman. That'll be tough. Guarding somebody out on the court will probably be his thing, too.

Warren Carter?

I've got to be cautious about what I say, but he could be really good. I talked to James Augustine, who we recruited at Southern. I asked him how he had so much success. He said, "No one expected anything out of me. I didn't have an ego like some of these guys. I thought I was going to redshirt, Coach. I just came out and busted my butt, and it just all happened." And I think that's how Warren is, too. He received the least attention. He's from Texas. He's very talented. He's a great kid and he just wants to learn. Our guards have to run the mile in 5:30 and he's six-foot-nine, and he made 5:30. He was second or third on the team. So, he can run. His thing will be his body. We'll see how things unfold. I need one of those guys to come through to give us a little more depth.

Do you set numerical goals?

I have usually set goals in the past. Not so much numbers, but championships, winning at these places, things like that. We have a difficult non-conference schedule—especially for a new coach. We're a talented team, but we're a young team. It could be a real challenge. You go to Temple and North Carolina. What are your odds of winning both games? What are the odds of winning one of two? Maybe you lose one and you lose some confidence. Does the coaching staff know what it's doing? So there's a lot of crazy things to consider. But on the other hand, I think in the long run it's going to help us be better prepared to go on the road in the Big Ten. I just don't like the setup. You shouldn't have two games like that on the road. It's what football's gone through. Old coaches have told me this, but I didn't understand 15 to 20 years ago. The two most important things you do in coaching are recruiting and scheduling. A lot of times how good you are depends on what you do with your schedule. Al Maguire, some of those old guys, they were masters at it. At Southern we didn't have a choice. We had to play anyone who would play us. No one would play us. Here, I'm hoping in the long run it'll help us.

Can this team win the Big Ten?

I think we have enough talent. We've got to buy into guarding somebody. Somebody in the post has to come through. And we have to have leadership and maturity. There are still some ifs, but I think we have enough talent. I really do. You've got to look at last year. Look at the road wins. It was at Penn State. They lost at Purdue, Indiana, Michigan State. They did win at Michigan, but they caught them at the end. And they almost beat Wisconsin. We've got to win some close games and some road games to have a chance to win it. We're going to be good, and if we answer some questions, we could be really good. Or, we could be a year away. We'll go through some growing pains, and that's what the trip to Europe helped with.

Where Have You Gone, Bruce Douglas?

Bruce Douglas, 39, was like a coach on the floor for Lou Henson's teams between 1982-86. The All-Stater from Quincy is the UI career leader in assists, steals, and minutes played, and averaged 10 points per game during his career. Today, he, his wife, Madge, and their four boys live in the Chicago area.

What are you doing these days?

I work full time for Exelon [Commonwealth Edison] as an operations manager. I'm also working on my Master's of Divinity at Moody Bible Institute. And, I'm a youth pastor at Broadview Missionary Baptist right outside of Maywood, Ill.. So, that takes up about 27 hours out of the day. I enjoy it though. I've had a chance to work in the business world and be in the ministry. I'd like to be in the ministry full time one day.

What's your greatest memory of your time spent at UI?

The most memorable event has to be winning the Big Ten during the 1983-84 season. Being a part of that team was really special. We had a lot of new players. It was a surprising team, but an exciting time. We had a four-overtime victory over Michigan and I played every minute of that one [an Illinois record].

What's the most significant thing that has happened for you since you left UI?

For me, it would definitely be going into the ministry. I was fortunate to get an education and play ball, but to minister and be a part of people coming to know the Lord has been a real benefit. Surely, marrying my wife is the most important thing, but the most significant thing is to be in ministry and serve my faith. It's a great privilege to help people.

What do you miss most about Champaign-Urbana?

It's an exciting place even though it's changed so much. I try to come down to at least one game a year. My kids are big U of I fans. When I stepped in the Assembly Hall last season it was emotional. I was talking to people about the privilege to play at the U of I. The program and education is second to none. Every time I get down there it just brings back great memories of a great time in my life.

Who's your favorite current Illini?

We know Dee because he played here on the west side. He's got a lot of heart, and I think he's going to be a great player. He's exciting, makes things happen. I think they have a great mixture of players. Some people have said to me that Deron reminds them of me. It's hard for me to measure myself against someone else, but I think he has a great court awareness and some good leadership qualities.

Have you met Coach Weber?

He recruited me while I was in high school. He was new at Purdue at the time. Bruce had called and visited. I had a good visit to Purdue. But my heart was always at Illinois. I think Weber's going to do a good job. I think the key, like for any good coach, is getting good players. He has a very good philosophy of the game, good structure, and he knows how to win. He has plenty of Big Ten experience, so I think the test will be to bring in players and win games.

Miss a day, miss a lot.

Will it pour?

Who's at war?

Don't be sore.

What's the score?

Try some more!

Who's on the floor?

Who's the mayor?

FORE!

Technology galore.

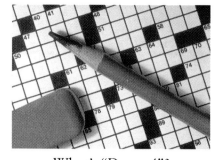

What's "Down 4"?

Will crop prices soar?

On the shore.

Need to know more? We deliver to your door!

CALL 1-800-660-READ TO SUBSCRIBE.

The News-Gazette
Living Life Today
www.news-gazette.com
© 2003 The News-Gazette, Inc.

An Off-season Rollercoaster Ride

By Doug Hoepker

The Fighting Illini off season began with a bang—or maybe that noise was a thud—following the completion of the 2002-03 season.

Rumors were buzzing around town like flies on a South Farms cow that Bill Self was considering taking the head coaching job at Kansas should Roy Williams leave the program for North Carolina. Amidst all the uncertainty and media frenzy, freshman forward and Texas-native Kyle Wilson, who averaged 2.6 points per game, quietly declared that he was transferring to Wichita State.

"With everything that happened this year, I was looking to get closer to home," said Wilson, who has family in the Wichita area.

Wilson's departure was the first shoe that dropped for the Illini this off season. It would pale in comparison, however, to the thunderous boom of the other shoe that days later would smack the pavement of Campustown on its way westward. Unfortunately, that shoe wasn't Brian Cook joining the Lakers.

Self Moves to Kansas

On April 21, 2003, less than a month after Illinois was eliminated by Notre Dame in the NCAA Tournament,

Bill Self announced he was leaving the program to take over the coaching reins at Kansas. Self amassed a 78-24 record after three seasons at the University of Illinois. That sparkling record earned him a .765 winning percentage, the second-highest mark ever for an Illini coach behind only Fletcher Lane's mark of .769 during his one season as head coach in 1908.

At the University of Kansas press conference announcing his hiring, Self expressed mixed emotions on his decision to bolt UI for KU.

"Nobody picks the timing and certainly I didn't pick this," Self said. "[My Illini family] is upset and they're mad and they're disappointed, and certainly any emotions that they have are warranted...There's great young players in the Illinois program and they're tough and they're competitive and they are unselfish and they sacrifice for the good of others and they understand what it takes to win at the highest level. They're going to be good no matter who's coaching them. Ron Guenther is a fabulous AD and he'll bring in the very best [to replace me]."

Self's departure left a gaping hole to be filled, and the hunt for a new coach—filled with speculation on some of the nation's top coaches—was on.

Bring Out the Welcome Wagon

It didn't take long for the DIA to reverse momentum and charge full-steam ahead.

Nine days after Self's departure became official, Guenther had his man: Southern Illinois University's Bruce Weber.

Weber had turned around a struggling SIU program that had compiled three-straight losing seasons prior to his five-year tenure. The 47-year-old coach joins the Illini after winning back-to-back Missouri Valley Conference titles and completing a pair of NCAA

Coach Weber at his press conference announcing him as Bill Self's successor at Illinois.

tournament runs that included a Sweet Sixteen appearance in 2002. Not only had Weber tallied 103 wins in five seasons at SIU—including 52 wins over his final two campaigns—but he also took home some hardware of his own after the 2003 season when he was named the Missouri Valley Conference Coach of the Year.

Weber's ties to the Big Ten Conference are strong. He spent 18 years as an assistant to Purdue coach Gene Keady. Many within the media thought he was a wise and obvious—not to mention safe—choice to follow Bill Self. The University of Illinois agreed.

Weber's exceptional reputation coupled with his Midwest roots and Big Ten experience made the decision an easy one for Guenther.

"I like Bruce a lot," Guenther said at the press conference announcing Weber as the new coach. "We want to raise the bar because we brought discipline to the program, we brought a lot of toughness to the program, and we brought some heart to the program."

At his press conference, Weber's confident demeanor exuded the excitement he felt from being named the University of Illinois' 16th men's basketball coach.

"I am honored and humbled to be named the coach at this institution," Weber said. "All coaches talk about dream jobs, and for me I had a dream of being a Big Ten coach—a head coach…This is an opportunity to be in a program that I truly believe is one of the top 15 in the country and truly has that chance to win a national championship."

Self felt the university made the right call in selecting his successor.

"Bruce Weber is a tremendous coach, and someone I have a great deal of respect for," Self commented. "We competed against his teams at both Tulsa and Illinois—we split those games, and we were lucky to do so."

Patriot Games

As Weber settled in to his new office at the Ubben facility and rallied together a support staff of assistant coaches, several returning members of the Fighting Illini had plans to do a little sightseeing over the summer.

James Augustine, Dee Brown and Deron Williams all attended the trials for the USA Basketball Men's National Team held in Colorado Springs, Colo., over the weekend of May 30. Joined by 44 other collegians, the players were vying for a spot on either the USA Basketball Junior World Championship Team or the USA Pan-American Games Team.

Brown and Williams both made the cut for the Junior World Championships squad after working out a second time at a training camp in Dallas, in late June.

Deron Williams
Photo courtesy of USA Basketball

Together with Oregon coach Ernie Kent and their 10 teammates, the duo dazzled fans on the international level en route to a fifth-place finish at the 2003 FIBA Junior World Championships held in Thessaloniki, Greece.

The only blemish on USA's 7-1 record was a 106-85 loss to Australia that cost them a chance at the gold medal. Due to the tournament's odd point system that factors in margin of defeat when considering which teams will advance to the medal round, the U.S. was held out of a medal game despite tying for the best overall record. Australia, who also finished 7-1, went on to defeat Lithuania 126-92 in the championship game.

Brown led the U.S. squad in minutes played per game and finished second in scoring average (17.3) to Michigan State's Paul Davis (17.7). Williams bested Brown in the assist column, leading the team in eight games with 38 assists to Brown's 33.

However, Brown earned the most face time on the highlight reels thanks to a record-setting 47-point game against Lithuania. In the game, Brown led the team to a comeback victory by tallying 19 of the team's 21 fourth-quarter points. Overall, Brown shot 18-of-29 from the field, drilled nine three-point baskets, and added six assists and six steals.

"Dee Brown saved us," Coach Kent said after the game. "I can't say enough about him."

Dee Brown

European Vacation

The sophomore duo was just receiving its first taste of international basketball during the 2003 summer. Brown and Williams would accompany new coach Weber and the other seven returning Fighting Illini for an 11-day trip through northern Europe. Incoming freshman players Richard McBride, Brian Randle, and Warren Carter were not eligible to travel with the team.

From August 9-19, the team went a perfect 6-0, battling Scandinavian counterparts in games held in Sweden, Estonia and Finland.

Luther Head nailed a three-pointer at the buzzer to seal a 110-109 victory over the Swedish University Games team in the opener. Brown, who was named as one of 50 preseason candidates for the Wooden Award, scored a team-best 28 points in the victory. Roger Powell chipped in 19 points and nine rebounds, while both Augustine and Aaron Spears grabbed 10 boards.

Moving from Stockholm to Sodertalje, Sweden, for game 2, the Fighting Illini again relied upon Brown's stellar shooting—including four three-pointers—to notch a 95-85 win over the Sodertalje Kings. Forward Jack Ingram, who redshirted last season, contributed 19 points and 12 rebounds, seven of which came on the offensive end.

Game 3 was a 100-90 win over the KTD-Kotka Tyovaen Palloilijat Basketball Club. (Try saying that 10 times fast.)

For game 4 the team traveled from Sweden to Kotka, Finland. Brown scored 26 points in the game—including 17 first-half points—in leading the Fighting Illini to victory. Augustine had a fine game as well, shooting 10 of 14 from the field in scoring 24 points. Powell earned a double-double for his efforts in collecting 13 rebounds and scoring 17 points.

After the game, Brown shared his enthusiasm for the team's performance.

"I am excited about this team and see a lot of potential," Brown said. "So far we have not played well defensively, and last year we were second in the nation in defensive field-goal percentage, so that has to improve."

Weber's SIU teams were renowned for their tough, aggressive defense.

"We've made progress on defense and in several stretches have really played well," related Weber. "What I'm looking for over the last three games is consistency."

The team boated across the Baltic Sea for Game 4, a match-up with Estonia's Kalev Tallinn Basketball Club. The Fighting Illini earned their first blowout of the trip with a 101-78 win.

"We were very balanced offensively tonight," said Weber of his team that featured six players scoring in double figures. "Deron [Williams] played very well on both ends of the court and shot the ball well."

Game 5 proved even easier for the Illini squad as they clobbered another Estonia team, Tallinn A. Le Coq Basketball Club, by the score of 101-67. Dee Brown led the way again with 19 points, and Augustine contributed his second double-double of the trip.

For the third-consecutive game, Illinois had six players score in double figures during Game 6, a 111-63 victory over Finland's Pussihukat Basketball Club. Powell posted 26 points and 10 rebounds in the win.

"The guys kept the focus of building on the improvement we made during the trip," said Weber. "We would have liked to have had some stronger opponents, but we played who was on the schedule."

All signs from the team's overseas trip point toward a positive transition from Coach Self's high-low offense to Coach Weber's motion offense. The team also handled the different international rules with ease. College basketball is expected to adopt the three-point line for the 2004-05 season.

"Overall, the trip was very positive," said Weber, concluding that it was a great learning experience for both the players and the new coaches. "Our players traveled very well and were great representatives of the University of Illinois."

Expectations are building for another exciting season of Fighting Illini basketball. With a host of new faces—and one familiar face in Brian Cook missing from the mix—it's not too far of a stretch to think that this Big Ten season will top the wild ride this off season has been.

The nine returning players of the men's basketball team (pictured in inset) headed to Scandinavia along with the new coaching staff for a six-game exhibition tour in August. The warm-up for the 2003-04 season provided the team with a bit of time for sightseeing in Stockholm.

SPEND YOUR SUMMER WITH THE FIGHTING ILLINI

Basketball Camps Run All Summer Long

June 4-5: Parent-Child 1
June 5-6: Parent-Child 2
June 11-12: Satellite Team Camp (Chicago)
June 13-16: Instructional Session 1
June 18-20: High School Team Camp
June 24-27: Instructional Session 2
June 25: Elite Camp
July 18-21: Day Camp

**CALL THE ILLINOIS SUMMER CAMP OFFICE AT
217/244-7278 FOR MORE INFORMATION**

A new era of Illini basketball gets underway in 2003-04 as Bruce Weber takes over a program coming off three Big Ten championships and a Big Ten Tournament title in the last six seasons.

Weber inherits a squad that ran off 25 wins a year ago with just one senior in the starting lineup. Of course, that one senior was Big Ten Player of the Year Brian Cook, who led the league in scoring at 20.0 points per game. A heralded freshman class is now one year older and more experienced after guards Dee Brown and Deron Williams and forward James Augustine combined for 95 starts during the season.

The new coach got an early look at his squad during a 10-day tour of Scandinavia, where the returning players won all six games.

"We're very talented physically," Weber said. "Even a person who doesn't know much about basketball can see Dee's quickness, Roger's and Luther's jumping ability, and the quantity of big bodies on this team. The thing we'll have to work on most is leadership and maturity on the floor with all the young guys. We have lots of guys who have played minutes, but their roles are different now than when they had Sean Harrington and Brian Cook to look to last season. Who's going to be the leader? Who's going to make the big shot? Who's going

Dee Brown

to be the defensive stopper? These are things I hope will work themselves out early in the season."

Brown and Williams figure to be one of the top backcourt tandems in the nation after finishing first and third, respectively, in assists in the Big Ten and ranking first and second in assist-to-turnover ratio.

Brown earned raves around the league on his way to second-team All-Big Ten honors. There is no wonder where he earned the nickname of "one-man fast break." Brown was second on the team in scoring at 12.0 points per game, while leading the team in assists (4.97 avg.) and steals (1.78). He also ranked third on the team in rebounding with an average of 3.7 boards per game. His 2.56 assist-to-turnover ratio led the league. Brown was named a preseason All-American by *Playboy Magazine*.

Although Williams didn't score at the same rate as Brown, his contribution to the team was equal. Williams quickly earned the reputation as the team's top defensive player, and finished third in the Big Ten in assists (4.53 avg.) and second in assist-to-turnover ratio (2.46). He finished the year averaging 6.3 points per game, but showed great flashes of improved shooting while playing for the USA Junior World Championship team over the summer.

James Augustine

"Each one of our guards is a little different," Weber said. "Dee has the jets. He just explodes with the basketball. He's so good in transition and, after this summer, feels more and more confident about his offensive game and scoring. Deron is a good all-around player. He passes very well. He's a great defender who has a big body and can guard a lot of positions. He's got to gain more confidence in his shooting ability."

Junior guard Luther Head hopes to rebound from an injury-plagued season in 2003. He missed seven games and played with pain for much of the year with a groin injury. Off-season surgery is expected to have Head back at 100 percent entering the 2003-04 season, which gives Illinois and Weber one of the top athletes in the Big Ten.

One of the best leapers in the nation, Head shot 52 percent from the field and averaged 7.9 points per game to rank fourth on the squad in scoring.

"A healthy Luther Head gives [us] another athletic guard, but I want him to be known for more than lob dunks. He needs to work on his pull-up jumpers and coming off screens looking for his shot. He's got a great mid-range game and I think the lack of practice last year with his injury did not allow his game to advance."

Junior Roger Powell is the fourth returning starter from a year ago. An athletic 6'6" guard/forward, Powell was exceptional down the stretch as he averaged 13.3 points in the final 11 games prior to the NCAA Tournament. In conference games only, he led the league in field-goal shooting at 64.1 percent, and finished second in all games at 59.1 percent. He was third on the team in scoring at 8.7 points and earned a spot on the Big Ten All-Tournament team.

Roger Powell

"Roger is a mismatch at the three position because he can go inside, he can rebound well and he's good in transition," Weber said. "You have a little different player in each one ... an explosive jumper ... your quick zipper... your solid, big-body guard, then Roger, who size-wise, is a matchup problem for most teams."

Guard Jerrance Howard returns as the only senior on the squad. He originally indicated last season that he would not return for his final season of eligibility, but changed his mind during the summer. Howard saw action in 14 games last season and gives the Illini added leadership from an upperclassman.

"Jerrance has been through it before," Weber said. "He wants to go into coaching, so hopefully he can give us some of the leadership we need."

Weber is looking at five players plus possibly Powell to provide strong inside play.

Augustine started all but three games and finished his first season averaging 7.0 points and 5.8 rebounds per game, while shooting 58 percent from the field. He showed great athleticism during the season and was a finalist for the U.S. Junior National Team along with Brown and Williams before withdrawing to concentrate on summer school and get stronger for his sophomore season.

Augustine joined Brown on the first-ever Big Ten All-Freshman team.

"James had a great freshman year," Weber said. "He can run and he jumps well. He just seems to be one of those kids who plays hard all the time. I want James to advance his game, develop his post moves and feel better about his jump shot."

Junior Nick Smith was solid during Big Ten play for the Illini, averaging 5.9 points and 2.9 rebounds, while shooting 67 percent from the field and 91 percent from the free-throw line. He led the Illini in blocked shots with 38 and enters his junior season with high expectations.

"Nick is a tall, lanky player with great skills," Weber said. "He can shoot very well, pass well and he has a good feel for the game. We want him to be more physical and rebound more."

Aaron Spears ended up playing just six games before suffering a knee injury that sidelined him the remainder of the year. He returns and adds much-needed bulk to the Illini interior game. Spears would definitely have been a factor for Illinois during Big Ten play if he had not been injured.

"Aaron was the biggest surprise on our trip to Europe," Weber said. "This fall is huge for him. He understands what we expect from him and I think he has a lot more confidence in himself."

Another newcomer to the floor is 6'10" junior Jack Ingram, who is eligible after transferring to Illinois from Tulsa in 2002. Ingram has shown great shooting ability and gives the Illini an additional physical presence in the middle.

"Jack was someone I didn't know much about [when I arrived], but he gives you a good body and he can also go out and shoot the ball," Weber said. "He showed a great nose for the ball on the offensive boards during the trip to Europe."

Weber will also be counting on the three freshmen joining the squad.

Richard McBride, a 6'3" shooting guard, was a three-time all-state selection and has shown to be an outstanding shooter. Extremely strong and powerful, McBride is expected to compete for playing time immediately.

Brian Randle is a slender 6'8" wing forward who is very athletic and has shown the ability to shoot the three-pointer. He also was a three-time All-Stater in Illinois and adds to the depth on the perimeter.

Nick Smith

Luther Head

Warren Carter was the Class 5A Player of the Year in Texas and could be the sleeper in the class. Very athletic at 6'9", Carter will battle for playing time along the Illini front line.

"He's long and lanky and a player who can run the court well, similar to Augustine," Weber said. "He can be in the mix, along with Roger, who can play the four. We have variety and should have good competition, for minutes and in practice."

Illinois again played one of the nation's toughest schedules last season and has several traditional powers on the 2003-04 slate as well. The Illini will take on Providence, North Carolina, Arkansas, Memphis, Illinois-Chicago, Temple and Missouri during the non-conference portion of the schedule before moving into the always-tough Big Ten.

"We have a challenging schedule this year which RPI-wise should be very high," Weber said. "We play some of the premier programs in the nation in non-conference play, which hopefully will make us ready for Big Ten play. It's also going to give us some neutral courts against quality opponents that will hopefully get us ready for the NCAA tournament."

Where Have You Gone, Jerry Hester?

Jerry Hester played for the Illini from 1993-98 and was a part of Lon Kruger's Big Ten champs during the 1997-98 season. The Peoria native averaged 11 points per game for his career and finished 12th on the all-time scoring list. He is currently playing professional basketball overseas.

What are you doing these days?

JH: I'm still playing basketball in Europe. I have played in a lot of different countries. I was even named MVP in a league in Poland.

What's your greatest memory of your time spent at UI?

JH: You know, when I left school I probably would have said winning the Big Ten in 1998 or the time we broke Duke's home winning streak against non-conference opponents. But now I would have to say the day I graduated. It will give me the opportunity to be successful when the ball stops bouncing.

Which of your former teammates do you stay in touch with?

JH: I have talked to pretty much everybody I played with since leaving, but on a consistent basis I would have to say T.J. Wheeler, Kiwane Garris, and Jarrod Gee.

What's the most significant thing that has happened for you since you left UI?

JH: I have two things that are most significant and both happened in August. The first happened on Aug. 17, 1998, the day I got married to my wife, Simone, who is also a graduate of Illinois. And the second is Aug. 12, 2000, the day my daughter, Jordyn Ella, came into this world. I will have a third significant day in March of 2004. My wife is pregnant with number two.

What do you miss most about Champaign-Urbana?

JH: I miss the great fans! I watch football games and the baseball playoffs now and see fans boo after one bad play. Illini fans are not like that! They were with us through good and bad, and that means a lot to an athlete.

Do you have a favorite Illini from the current team?

JH: I don't really have a favorite Illini, because I'm not able to watch games overseas. My schedule is during the same time as the collegiate and pro schedule here. All I can say is keep winning so I can continue to have bragging rights whenever I run into former Big Ten players from other schools.

Have you met Coach Weber?

JH: I had the opportunity to meet Coach Weber, and talk to him at length. I really believe he is going to continue to have success, and the Illini fans will be very proud of the job he and his staff will do.

2003-04 Fighting Illini Roster

No.	Name	Pos.	Ht.	Wt.	Year	Hometown/HS/Previous College
1	Aaron Spears	F/C	6'9"	260	Fr.-r	Chicago, Ill./Dunbar HS
4	Luther Head	G	6'3"	175	Jr.	Chicago, Ill./Manley HS
5	Deron Williams	G	6'3"	210	So.	The Colony, Texas/The Colony HS
11	Dee Brown	G	6'0"	177	So.	Maywood, Ill./Proviso East HS
25	Jerrance Howard	G	6'1"	200	Sr.-r	Peoria, Ill./Peoria HS
33	Richard McBride	G	6'3"	210	Fr.	Springfield, Ill./Lanphier HS
40	James Augustine	F	6'10"	225	So.	Mokena, Ill./Lincoln-Way Central HS
41	Warren Carter	F	6'9"	205	Fr.	Dallas, Texas/Lake Highlands HS
42	Brian Randle	F	6'8"	200	Fr.	Peoria, Ill./Notre Dame HS
43	Roger Powell	F	6'6"	220	Jr.	Joliet, Ill./Joliet HS
45	Nick Smith	C	7'2"	240	Jr.-r	Valrico, Fla./Bloomingdale HS
50	Jack Ingram	F/C	6'10"	240	Jr.-r	San Antonio, Texas/Marshall HS/Tulsa

Head Coach

Bruce Weber (first year at Illinois, 103-54 in his sixth year as a collegiate head coach)

Assistant Coaches

Chris Lowery, Wayne McClain, Jay Price

Administrative Assistant

Gary Nottingham

Director of Basketball Operations

Rod Cardinal

Trainer

Al Martindale

James Augustine

Sophomore Forward • 6'10" • 225

AT ILLINOIS

2003-2004 Sophomore:

Averaged 12.7 points and 7.2 rebounds during the six-game team trip to Scandinavia in August, shooting 66 percent from the field ... One of 18 finalists selected for the USA Basketball Men's National Team Trials along with teammates Dee Brown and Deron Williams.

2002-2003 Freshman:

Named to first-ever Big Ten All-Freshman Team ... Started 29 of 32 games ... Second on the team in field goal percentage, shooting 58.0 percent (94-162) ... Ranked third in the Big Ten in field goal percentage during conference play at 58.6 percent (51-87) ... Second on the team in rebounding, averaging 5.8 boards (13th in Big Ten) ... Led the Illini with 64 offensive rebounds ... Second on the team in blocked shots with 27 (13th in Big Ten) ... Recorded a double-double in the Big Ten Tournament championship game vs. Ohio State with 12 points and 10 boards ... Recorded his first career double-double at Penn State, scoring a career-high 19 points and pulling down a career-high 12 rebounds ... Also recorded a double-double vs. Michigan with 11 points and 10 boards ... Scored 17 points on 8-of-10 shooting vs. Wisconsin ... Scored in double figures nine times ... Illinois' leading rebounder in nine games ... Had a career-high five blocks vs. Oakland, tying the most by a UI player during the season.

High School

Mokena, Ill./Lincoln-Way Central H.S.
Earned First-Team All-State honors from the Champaign-Urbana *News-Gazette* after averaging 18 points, 10.6 rebounds and four blocked shots per game ... Averaged 14 points, seven rebounds and five blocks as a junior ... Burst on the scene while earning All-Star honors at the Adidas ABCD camp in the summer before his senior season ... Consensus Top 100 recruit nationally ... Team finished the year 25-5, advancing to the super-sectional (Sweet Sixteen) of the IHSA Class AA State Tournament ... Ranked by All-Star Report as the No. 69 player in the nation ... Also ranked No. 69 by RivalsHoops.com...Ranked No. 71 by Blue Chip Hoops ... Selected to play in the Wendy's Shootout, an All-Star game featuring preps from the Chicago area vs. the New York City area ... Played in the IBCA All-Star game ... Multi-sport athlete also played football (lettered in 2001 at quarterback) and baseball (lettered in 2001 and 2002 as a pitcher) at Lincoln-Way Central.

Personal

Born Feb. 27, 1984 ... Parents are Dale and Barb Augustine ... Was a quarterback on the Lincoln-Way football team until his senior year when he concentrated on basketball ... Played football under his father Dale ... High school basketball coach was Steve Little ... Nickname is Augie ...Uncle Jerry Augustine played professional baseball in the Milwaukee Brewers' organization from 1973-85 ... Uncle Dick Sorensen played football for the Miami Hurricanes from 1965-70 while cousin, Nick Sorensen played football at Virginia Tech from 1995-2000 and with the St. Louis Rams ... Father Dale played collegiately at Wisconsin-Oshkosh while his mother, Barb, was a swimmer for the Titans ... Majoring in sport management.

AUGUSTINE'S CAREER STATS

Year	G-GS	MIN-Avg	FGM-A/%	3PM-A/%	FTM-A/%	OR-DR—TOT/Avg	PF-DQ	A	TO	B	S	PTS/Avg
02-03	32-29	697-21.8	94-162/.580	5-14/.357	32-45/.711	64-122—186/5.8	105-5	25	45	27	20	225/7.0
Total	**32-29**	**697-21.8**	**94-162/.580**	**5-14/.357**	**32-45/.711**	**64-122—186/5.8**	**105-5**	**25**	**45**	**27**	**20**	**225/7.0**

CAREER
Highs

Points *19*
vs. Penn State (1/25/03)

FG *9*
vs. Penn State (1/25/03)

FGA *14*
vs. Penn State (1/25/03)

3P .... *1, five times*
last vs. Michigan (3/1/03)

3PA *2*
vs. Michigan (3/1/03)

FT *5*
vs. Michigan (1/29/03)

FTA *6*
vs. Michigan (1/29/03)

Rebounds *12*
vs. Penn State (1/25/03)

Assists *4*
vs. Arkansas-Pine Bluff
(11/27/02)

Blocks *5*
vs. Oakland (1/4/03)

Steals *3*
vs. Indiana (3/14/03)

Minutes *34*
vs. Purdue (1/22/03)

Dee Brown

Sophomore Guard • 6'0" • 177

AT ILLINOIS

2003-2004 Sophomore:
Preseason *Playboy Magazine* All-America selection ... Led the USA Basketball Men's National Junior Team in scoring with a 17.3 average and in steals with 19 during the summer ... Set a U.S. Junior World Championships team record with 47 points in 87-84 win over Lithuania ... Along with teammate Deron Williams, helped the U.S. to a fifth-place finish in Greece with a 7-1 record ... Averaged a team-high 21.5 points while shooting 54 percent from the field on Illinois' six-game Scandinavian tour in August.

2002-2003 Freshman: Second-Team All-Big Ten selection by the media and Third-Team All-Big Ten by league coaches ... Named to first-ever Big Ten All-Freshman Team ... Started 31 of 32 games at guard, leading the team in minutes played at 34.1 mpg ... Second on the team in scoring, averaging 12.0 points ... Scored in double figures in 19 games, with four 20-plus point performances (career-high 25 vs. Eastern Illinois) ... Led the Big Ten (all games) in assists, averaging 4.97 per game ... His total of 159 assists ranks seventh on the Illinois single-season assists list ... Finished second in the league in assists in conference games with 76, falling just one assist shy of teammate Deron Williams for the Big Ten lead ... Led the Big Ten in steals in conference games, averaging 1.9 steals per game and finished third in all games with average of 1.78 ... Big Ten leader in assist-to-turnover ratio in all games (+2.56) and conference games (+3.04) ... Reached double figures in assists twice, with 10 vs. Western Illinois and career-high 11 at Penn State ... Became the first freshman in Illinois history to earn Big Ten Player of the Week honors after scoring 21 points against No. 11 Missouri, adding a game-high seven assists and five rebounds, including four offensive ... One of 12 players on the 2002 USA Basketball Men's Junior World Championship Qualifying Team ... Helped the U.S. to a bronze medal along with fellow Illini Deron Williams.

High School
Maywood, Ill./Proviso East H.S.
Earned Mr. Basketball honors in state of Illinois following his senior season ... The ninth Mr. Basketball to attend Illinois since the award began in 1981 ... Named Illinois' Gatorade Player of the Year in 2002 ... McDonald's All-American ... Champaign-Urbana *News-Gazette* Illinois Player of the Year in 2002 ... First-team All-State pick by the IBCA, *Chicago Tribune*, Chicago *Sun-Times*, Champaign-Urbana *News-Gazette* ... Finished his high school career as Proviso East's all-time leader in scoring, assists and steals. Averaged 25.6 points, 5.5 assists and 2.9 steals per game as a senior ... Made 12 three-pointers on his way to 42 points against Addison Trail High School as a senior ... Helped the Pirates to the Sweet Sixteen of the Illinois state tournament as a senior ... Ranked by RivalsHoops.com as the No. 2 point guard and No. 11 player overall in the nation ... Ranked the No. 3 point guard and No. 18 player overall by Blue Chip Hoops ... Ranked by All-Star Report as the nation's No. 19 player ... Also played football at Proviso East, starting at quarterback and lettering in 2000 and 2001 ... Passed and ran for more than 1,800 yards and 16 touchdowns in seven games as a quarterback during his senior season and earned recruiting overtures from Florida State and Nebraska for football.

Personal

Born Aug. 17, 1984, in Jackson, Miss. ... Mother is Cathy Brown-Blocker ... Father is Fred Brown ... Given name is Daniel ... Nicknamed "The One-Man Fast Break" ... Coached by Troy Jackson as a senior at Proviso East ... Had a class rank of 16 out of 382 in his senior class ... Attended the same high school as former NBA player and current NBA coach Glenn "Doc" Rivers ... Favorite athlete is NBA star Allen Iverson ... Majoring in sport management.

BROWN'S CAREER STATS

Year	G-GS	MIN-Avg	FGM-A/%	3PM-A/%	FTM-A/%	OR-DR—TOT/Avg	PF-DQ	A	TO	B	S	PTS/Avg
02-03	32-31	1090-34.1	142-327/.434	51-155/.329	49-72/.681	35-84—119/3.7	56-0	159	62	0	57	384/12.0
Totals	**32-31**	**1090-34.1**	**142-327/.434**	**51-155/.329**	**49-72/.681**	**35-84—119/3.7**	**56-0**	**159**	**62**	**0**	**57**	**384/12.0**

CAREER
Highs

Points **25**
vs. Eastern Illinois
(12/10/02)

FG **10**
vs. Eastern Illinois
(12/10/02)

FGA **17**
vs. Wisconsin (3/5/03)

3P .... *5, three times*
last vs. Indiana (1/18/03)

3PA **11**
vs. Memphis (12/28/02)

FT **6**
vs. Michigan State
(2/18/03)

FTA **8**
vs. Michigan State (2/18/03)

Rebounds **7**
vs. Western Kentucky
(3/20/03)

Assists **11**
vs. Penn State (1/25/03)

Blocks **0**

Steals .... *5, twice*
vs. Michigan State
(2/18/03) & vs.
Northwestern (2/22/03)

Minutes... 39, three times
last vs. Wisconsin (3/5/03)

Luther Head

Junior Guard • 6'3" • 175

AT ILLINOIS

2003-04 Junior: Averaged a fourth-best 12.7 points during Illinois' six-game tour through Scandinavia in August ... Hit game-winning three-pointer at buzzer in overtime in Illinois' 110-109 victory over the Swedish University Games team.

2002-03 Sophomore: Pelvic injury slowed him during the season and caused him to miss seven games, but he still started eight games and played more than 20 minutes per contest ... Shot 58.5 percent (24 of 41) from the floor in his last 10 games and hit 48 percent (12-of-25) of his shots from beyond the arc in his last 11 ... Fourth on the team in scoring, averaging 7.9 points ... Shot 42.4 percent from three-point land (28 of 66) ... Also hit 51.9 percent of his shots from the floor (68-131) ... Scored in double figures nine times, including five times during Big Ten play ... Scored a season-high 16 points in the Big Ten Tournament semifinal win over Indiana ... Averaged 11.0 points in Illinois' three Big Ten Tournament victories while hitting 69.2 percent of his shots ... Scored 15 points against Purdue, hitting five of nine shots and three three-pointers ... Also had three makes from beyond the arc at Michigan State.

2001-02 Freshman: True freshman started 13 games, including 11 of the last 12, and averaged 4.5 points in 16.6 minutes per game ... Second on the team with 34 steals ... Shot 51 percent from the field (63 of 124) ... Scored a career-high 19 points in NCAA Tournament first-round win over San Diego State, hitting eight of 11 shots, including three treys ... Also tallied four assists and three steals against the Aztecs ... Dished out a career-high six assists vs. Kansas in Sweet Sixteen ... Scored 14 points twice, against Eastern Illinois and Western Illinois ... Hit seven of nine shots against EIU and made a season-high three treys against WIU ...

Scored 13 points against Michigan on perfect five for five shooting, including two of two on three-pointers.

High School
Chicago, Ill./Manley H.S.

Averaged 22 points, eight rebounds, six assists and five steals in the rugged Red-West Division of the Chicago Public League ... Earned First-Team All-State honors in 2001 from the *Chicago Tribune*, Chicago *Sun-Times*, Champaign-Urbana *News-Gazette*, Associated Press and Illinois Basketball Coaches Association ... Played in the Wendy's All-Star Classic ... First Illinois recruit out of the Chicago Public League since 1994 ... Finished sixth in voting for Mr. Basketball in Illinois following his senior season ... Averaged more than 20 points, eight assists and seven rebounds per game as a junior at Manley Academy ... Earned All-City honors and was the MVP of the Blue Division of the Chicago Public League ... Led Manley to a perfect 12-0 record and conference championship in the Blue-West ... Manley finished 26-7 overall, losing to state runner-up Chicago Westinghouse in the Public League quarterfinals ... Posted 10 triple-doubles during the season ... Broke the city record and recorded second highest number of assists in a game with 25 vs. Chicago Wells, earning Prep Player of the Week Honors from the *Chicago Tribune* ... Also named Gatorade Prep Player of the Week for his record-setting performance ... Had more than 20 points and 15 assists vs. Marshall in a first-round playoff victory, then posted a triple-double in a second-round win over Steinmetz ... Played point guard, shooting guard and small forward during the course of the season for Manley ... Attended Adidas ABCD Camp in New Jersey.

Personal

Born Nov. 26, 1982 ... The son of Bonnie Gallion ... Has four younger brothers and sisters ... Member of the volunteer organization Young Life ... High school coach was Bo Delaney ... Majoring in sport management.

HEAD'S CAREER STATISTICS

Year	G-GS	MIN-Avg	FGM-A/%	3PM-A/%	FTM-A/%	OR-DR—TOT/Avg	PF-DQ	A	TO	B	S	PTS/Avg
01-02	35-13	581-16.6	63-124/.508	16-55/.291	14-25/.560	17-50—67/1.9	55-1	59	43	5	34	156/4.5
02-03	25-8	509-20.4	68-131/.519	28-66/.424	34-46/.739	23-48—71/2.8	42-1	42	40	3	27	198/7.9
Total	**60-21**	**1090-18.2**	**131-255/.514**	**44-121/.364**	**48-71/.676**	**40-98—138/2.3**	**97-2**	**101**	**83**	**8**	**61**	**354/5.9**

CAREER
Highs

Points 19
vs. San Diego State
(3/15/02)

FG 8
vs. San Diego State
(3/15/02)

FGA 11
vs. San Diego State
(3/15/02)

3P ....*3, four times*
last vs. Michigan State
(2/2/03)

3PA .... *6, twice*
vs. San Diego State
(3/15/02) &
vs. Purdue (1/22/03)

FT 4
vs. Wisconsin (1/11/03)

FTA ....*4, six times*
last vs. Indiana (1/18/03)

Rebounds 7
vs. Ohio State (2/9/03)

Assists 6
vs. Kansas (3/22/02)

Blocks ....*1, six times*
last vs. Wisconsin (3/5/03)

Steals........................... 4
vs. Illinois State (12/18/01)

Minutes....................... 32
vs. Penn State (1/25/03)

Jerrance Howard

Senior Guard • 6'1" • 200

AT ILLINOIS

2003-04 Senior: After announcing that 2003 would be his last season, changed his mind and decided to return for his senior season in 2003-04.

2002-03 Junior: Saw action in 14 games and earned the first start of his collegiate career on Senior Day vs. Minnesota ... Saw action in six Big Ten contests ... Scored a career-high-tying four points on two of three shooting vs. Indiana ... Had three points and two assists vs. Minnesota ... Dished out a season-high three assists in eight minutes of action vs. Oakland ... Played a season-high nine minutes vs. Northwestern in the Big Ten Tournament quarterfinal.

2001-02 Sophomore: Reserve point guard played in 21 games on the year ... Scored season-high four points against Eastern Illinois, also tying his career high ... Played a season-high 10 minutes three times, against Georgia Tech, Western Illinois and Penn State ... Dished out career-high four assists against Western Illinois ... Tied career high with four points in NCAA tournament first-round win over San Diego State, hitting career-high two field goals.

2000-01 Freshman: Spelled Frank Williams as a backup point guard and saw action in 25 games ... Had season-high four assists vs. Wisconsin-Milwaukee ... Scored career-high four points against Penn State.

1999-2000: Sat out the season as a redshirt after becoming eligible midway through the season.

High School

Peoria, Ill./Peoria H.S.

Averaged 10.0 points, 7.8 assists and 4.0 rebounds as a senior at Peoria High School...A four-year basketball letterman ...Helped lead Peoria to a 23-4 record...Shot 47.5 percent from the field (85-of-179), and 31 percent from three-point range (9-of-29)...A 70 percent free-throw shooter (37-of-53)...Second-Team All-State selection (Illinois Basketball Coaches Association, *News-Gazette*) ... Third-Team All-State selection (Associated Press) ... First-Team All-Conference all four years of high school ...Chosen for the Peoria Area Top five list ... Played for Coach chuck Buescher ...Verbally committed to Illinois as a junior, signed with the Illini in the fall signing period.

Personal

Born May 28, 1980 ... Son of Al and Mary Hopson ... Has six brothers and one sister ... Chosen as Homecoming King as a senior ... A member of student council and the junior leadership program ... Peoria's junior class president and a Senior Ambassador ... One of many Michael Jordan fans on the Illini team, Jerrance likes the former NBA All-Star because of his hard work and love for the game ... Played one year in high school with former Indiana University star A.J. Guyton ... Majoring in speech communications.

HOWARD'S CAREER STATISTICS

Year	G-GS	MIN-Avg	FGM-A/%	3PM-A/%	FTM-A/%	OR-DR—TOT/Avg	PF-DQ	A	TO	B	S	PTS/Avg
00-01	25-0	85-3.4	4-15/.267	0-1/.000	2-4/.500	2-7—9/0.4	12-0	10	7	1	0	10/0.4
01-02	21-0	81-3.9	7-18/.389	2-7/.286	4-4/1.000	6-7—13/0.6	16-0	14	11	0	4	20/1.0
02-03	14-1	52-3.7	4-16/.250	1-6/.167	0-0/.000	0-3—3/0.2	5-0	7	2	0	0	9/0.6
Total	**60-1**	**218-3.6**	**15-49/.306**	**3-14/.214**	**6-8/.750**	**8-17—25/0.4**	**33-0**	**31**	**20**	**1**	**4**	**39/0.7**

CAREER
Highs

Points ....**4, four times**
last vs. Indiana (2/25/03)

FG ....**2, twice**
vs. San Diego State
(3/15/02) & vs. Indiana
(2/25/03)

FGA.................................**4**
vs. Northwestern (3/14/03)

3P..............**1, three times**
last vs. Minnesota (3/9/03)

3PA **3**
vs. Northwestern (3/14/03)

FT..............**2, three times**
last vs. Michigan (1/12/02)

FTA ....**2, four times**
last vs. Michigan (1/12/02)

Rebounds...........**3, twice**
vs. Maine (11/17/00) & vs.
Wisconsin (1/23/02)

Assists ....**4, twice**
vs. Wisconsin-Milwaukee
(12/6/00) & vs. Western
Illinois (12/16/01)

Blocks **1**
vs. Texas Southern
(11/26/00)

Steals..........**1, four times**
last vs. Michigan (1/12/02)

Minutes........................**12**
vs. Wisconsin-Milwaukee
(12/6/00)

Roger Powell

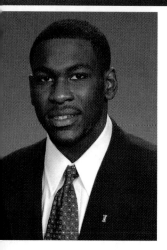

Junior Forward • 6'6" • 220

AT ILLINOIS

2003-04 Junior: Averaged 17.2 points (second highest) and team-high 8.7 rebounds on Illini's six-game Scandinavian tour in August.

2002-03 Sophomore: Named to the Big Ten All-Tournament Team after leading Illinois with 16 points in the Tournament title game vs. Ohio State and scoring 14 vs. Northwestern in the quarterfinals ... Started 19 games during the season including 10 of the last 11 ... Finished second in the Big Ten in field goal percentage in all games, hitting 59.1 percent from the field (104-176) ... Led the Big Ten in field goal percentage in conference games, connecting on 64.1 percent of his shots (50-78) ... Third on the team in scoring, averaging 8.7 points ... One of the hottest players down the stretch in the Big Ten, he averaged 13.3 points the last 11 games prior to the NCAA Tournament ... Scored a career-high 22 points vs. Indiana on nine of 13 shooting ... Had 20 points vs. Northwestern ... Tallied 18 points and seven rebounds at Michigan ... Scored in double figures 13 times, while scoring 15-plus points nine times ... Started the first nine contests of the season before suffering a toe injury that forced him out of the line up the next two weeks ... Traveled to Europe over the 2002 summer with the Big Ten Men's Basketball Foreign Tour team, leading the squad in scoring at 14.0 points per game.

2001-02 Freshman: True freshman played in 27 games on the year, averaging 2.9 points and 1.8 rebounds per game ... Scored season-high 12 points against Western Illinois, hitting four field goals and adding four free throws ... Gave Illinois a spark off the bench at Wisconsin, scoring six points on three-of-three shooting while grabbing four rebounds (three offensive).

High School
Joliet, Ill./Joliet H.S.

Earned First-Team All-State honors at Joliet in 2001 from the *Chicago Tribune*, Chicago *Sun-Times*, Champaign-Urbana *News-Gazette*, Associated Press and Illinois Basketball Coaches Association ... Also earned First-Team All-State honors in 2000 from the Champaign-Urbana *News-Gazette*, *Chicago Tribune* and Chicago *Sun-Times* ... A consensus Top 100 prospect ... Fourth in voting for Mr. Basketball in Illinois following his senior season ... Played in the Wendy's All-Star Classic and IBCA All-Star game following his senior year ... Earned MVP honors at the IBCA All-Star game... Averaged 20.7 points and nine rebounds for a 25-5 sectional finalist that was ranked No. 3 in the Chicago area as a senior ... As a junior, averaged 19 points and eight rebounds in leading the Steelmen to a 20-8 mark ... Second-Team All-State by AP and Illinois Basketball Coaches Association as a junior ... Three-year starter and four-year letterwinner ... Also as a junior, earned a bronze medal as a member of the 1999 USA Basketball Men's Youth Development Festival North Team ... Recorded Festival bests with 16 points vs. the East in the bronze medal game and seven rebounds vs. the South.

Personal

Born Jan. 15, 1983 ... Son of Cherry and Roger Powell ... Father was former Joliet Central and Illinois State University star ... High school coach was Bob Koskosky ... National Honor Society member ... Member of the Honor Roll all four years of high school ... Hugh O'Brien Youth Leadership Award winner ... Was Homecoming King as a senior and starred in the school musical as a junior and senior ... Cousin David Evans played basketball at Colorado State ... Majoring in speech communications.

POWELL'S CAREER STATISTICS

Year	G-GS	MIN-Avg	FGM-A/%	3PM-A/%	FTM-A/%	OR-DR—TOT/Avg	PF-DQ	A	TO	B	S	PTS/Avg
01-02	27-0	160-5.9	27-50/.540	3-5/.600	22-36/.611	19-29—48/1.8	21-0	2	10	4	3	79/2.9
02-03	30-19	558-18.6	104-176/.591	20-49/.408	33-57/.579	40-61—101/3.4	46-0	12	24	12	9	261/8.7
Total	**57-19**	**718-12.6**	**131-226/.580**	**23-54/.426**	**55-93/.591**	**59-90—149/2.6**	**67-0**	**14**	**34**	**16**	**12**	**340/6.0**

CAREER
Highs

Points 22
vs. Indiana (2/25/03)

FG 9
vs. Indiana (2/25/03)

FGA 13
vs. Indiana (2/25/03)

3P .... *2,six times*
last vs. Northwestern
(3/14/03)

3PA 5
vs. Lehigh (11/24/02)

FT 5
vs. Penn State (2/20/02)

FTA 9
vs. Penn State (2/20/02)

Rebounds 9
vs. Lehigh (11/24/02)

Assists 3
vs. Michigan (3/1/03)

Blocks .... *2, twice*
vs. Memphis (12/28/02) &
vs. Purdue (2/15/03)

Steals 4
vs. Missouri (12/21/02)

Minutes 32
vs. Northwestern (2/22/03)

Nick Smith

Junior Center • 7'2" • 240

AT ILLINOIS

2003-04 Junior: Averaged 6.2 points and 3.7 rebounds while shooting 52 percent from the field during Illini's six-game Scandinavian tour in August.

2002-03 Sophomore: Academic All-Big Ten selection ... Shot 66.7 percent (34-of-51) from the field over his last 16 games of the season ... Made 67.3 percent of his shots (33-of-49) during Big Ten play ... Led the Illini in free-throw shooting at 86.4 percent (38-44) ... Shot 45.5 percent from beyond the arc (5-11) ... Led the team and ranked seventh in the Big Ten in blocked shots with 38 (1.23 bpg) ... Great passing big man who had 26 assists ... Scored in double figures four times during the season ... Scored a season-high 13 points at Indiana ... Scored 10 points on four of four shooting at Penn State, while also dishing out a career-high four assists ... Hit four of five shots including a three pointer in the win over Michigan State ... Had a career-high five blocks vs. Minnesota, tying the most by an Illini player this season ... Hit all five of his shots while blocking three shots in the Big Ten Tournament quarterfinal win over Northwestern ... Set a Big Ten Tournament record with eight blocked shots in the three games.

2001-02 Freshman: Academic All-Big Ten selection ... Played in 33 of 35 games, starting four times ... Averaged 3.8 points on 54 percent shooting from the field (49-of-91 FGs) ... Earned his first career start against Loyola-Chicago, responding with career bests of 17 points and nine rebounds against the Ramblers ... Scored in double figures three times ... Led Illinois in rebounding three times, against Western Illinois, Loyola and Minnesota ...Third on the team with 19 blocked shots ... Scored seven points and had four rebounds in Big Ten Tournament quarterfinals vs. Minnesota ... Traveled to England and Ireland as part of

the Big Ten tour team, helping the Big Ten squad to a perfect 6-0 record.

2000-01 Redshirt Season: Sat out the season as a redshirt. Retained four years of eligibility.

High School
Valrico, Fla./Bloomingdale H.S.
Florida Gatorade Player of the Year in 2000 ... Second-Team All-State selection as a senior after being named honorable-mention All-State as a junior ... First-Team All-Conference and All-Hillsborough County performer as a senior ... Averaged 25 points, 14 rebounds and five blocks as a senior ... Averaged 17 points, 15 rebounds and eight blocks as a junior ... High school coach was Jack Sutter ... Lettered four years in basketball ... Member of the 1999 USA Basketball Men's Youth Development Festival South Team that earned a 5-0 record en route to the gold medal, ranked as the Festival's eighth leading rebounder (6.0 rpg).

Personal

Born Sept. 25, 1982...Son of Nick and Donna Smith ... Was an academic letterman twice in high school ... Played in the Hillsborough County All-Star game ... Favorite athlete is Shaquille O'Neal "because I've never seen a single player totally dominate a game like he does, not even Jordan" ... The first seven-footer to sign with Illinois since Jens Kujawa in 1985...Born in Louisville, Ky. ... Grandparents, Odell and Edith Moseley, live in the Southern Illinois town of Alto Pass....Odell is a former school administrator in Champaign... Has traveled to Europe as part of high school all-star team ... The tallest player in University of Illinois basketball history, he is just the fourth seven-footer to play for Illinois following Bill Rucks (7-0, lettered 1973-76), Olaf Blab (7-0, never lettered) and Jens Kujawa (7-0, lettered 1986-88) ... Majoring in business finance.

SMITH'S CAREER STATISTICS

Year	G-GS	MIN-Avg	FGM-A/%	3PM-A/%	FTM-A/%	OR-DR—TOT/Avg	PF-DQ	A	TO	B	S	PTS/Avg
01-02	33-4	334-10.1	49-91/.538	0-3/.000	29-44/.659	26-48—74/2.2	51-1	20	28	19	5	127/3.8
02-03	31-5	539-17.4	60-121/.496	5-11/.455	38-44/.864	23-69—92/3.0	64-2	26	42	38	11	163/5.3
Total	**64-9**	**873-13.6**	**109-212/.514**	**5-14/.357**	**67-88/.761**	**49-117—166/2.6**	**115-3**	**46**	**70**	**57**	**16**	**290/4.5**

CAREER
Highs

Points 17
vs. Loyola-Chicago
(12/29/01)

FG .... 5, twice
last vs. Northwestern
(3/14/03)

FGA ....8, four times
last vs. North Carolina
(12/3/02)

3P .... 1, five times
last vs. Minnesota (3/9/03)

3PA .... 1, 14 times
last vs. Minnesota (3/9/03)

FT 9
vs. Loyola-Chicago
(12/29/01)

FTA 10
vs. Loyola-Chicago
(12/29/01)

Rebounds 9
vs. Loyola-Chicago
(12/29/01)

Assists 4
vs. Penn State (1/25/03)

Blocks 5
vs. Minnesota (3/9/03)

Steals .... 2, twice
vs. Wisconsin (1/23/02) &
vs. Michigan State (2/18/03)

Minutes 30
vs. Loyola-Chicago
(12/29/01)

NOTHING BUT NYLON BABY!

Go Illini!

Photo courtesy of Dick Vitale.

A REAL DIPSY-DOO DUNKAROO!

A SAMPLE FROM *DICK VITALE'S LIVING A DREAM*

"Everybody's buddy."

That phrase has always summarized my personality.

You've seen it in the studio.

Like the time Austin Peay played Illinois in the 1987 NCAA Tournament. We're doing cutaways to different games. Bob Ley was there, along with producer Steve Anderson. And we're all trying to have a little fun in the studio. I felt like Austin Peay had no shot, and I said so: "I'm going to tell you now. Austin Peay has no shot.

"This is a total M&Mer," I said. "If they win, I'll stand on my head."

And then the score comes in. Man, the phones started ringing off the hook— "He'd better stand on his head."

Well, I'd said I would, hadn't I? So I let the guys stand me on my head on the desk in front of the camera. It was a riot.

Hey, I did it again at Austin Peay later on, when they invited me to be the keynote speaker at their basketball banquet.

I was amazed. They let loose on me with this cheer: "Let's go, Peay. Let's go, Peay—On Vitale. On Vitale."

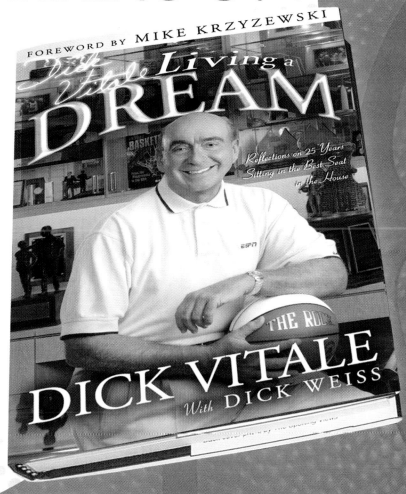

DICK VITALE'S LIVING A DREAM
Reflections on 25 Years Sitting in the Best Seat in the House

by Dick Vitale with Dick Weiss
Foreword by Mike Krzyzewski

Aaron Spears

Freshman Center • 6'9" • 260

AT ILLINOIS

2003-2004 Freshman Redshirt: Averaged 7.7 points and 8.0 rebounds (second best on team) during Illinois' six-game Scandinavian tour in August.

2002-2003 Freshman: As a true freshman played in the first six games of the season before suffering a torn lateral meniscus in his left knee during practice on Dec. 16 ... Had arthroscopic surgery on Dec. 27 and applied for a medical redshirt after the season to preserve a year of eligibility ... Averaged 3.2 points and 1.5 rebounds before the injury ... Scored a career-high eight points vs. Arkansas-Pine Bluff.

High School

Chicago, Ill./Dunbar H.S.
Earned First-Team All-State honors from the Chicago *Sun-Times* and Champaign-Urbana *News-Gazette* after averaging 26 points and 12 rebounds, two blocks and three assists per game ... Also earned Special-Mention All-State honors by the *Chicago Tribune* and Honorable-Mention All-State by the Associated Press ... First-team All-City by the *Chicago Tribune* and Chicago *Sun-Times* ... Chicago Public League Red Central Division MVP ... Played in the Michael Jordan Capital Classic All-Star game with fellow Illini recruit Dee Brown ... Also played in the Wendy's Classic, the New York-Chicago Challenge as well as Chicago's City vs. Suburban game and the IBCA All-Star game ... Helped Dunbar to the Chicago Public League Final Four in 2001.

Personal

Born Feb. 2, 1984 in Chicago ... Mother is Bonnie Spears ... Father Dan Davis was an all-state player at Crane High School in 1965 who later went on to play at Northwestern from 1967-69, earning Academic All-Big Ten honors in 1968 and leading the Wildcats in free-throw shooting in 1969 (.882), which still stands as the third-best season in NU history ... Davis later coached at Crane, which he guided to the 1972 state finals, and at Malcolm X Junior College ... High school coach was Fate Mickel ... Nickname is "Big Aaron" ... Favorite athlete is NBA star Kevin Garnett ... Mentions Floyd Fulton as the person who most influenced his athletic career because, "He provided a gym for me to play in anytime I needed." ... Majoring in speech communications.

SPEARS'S CAREER STATISTICS

Year	G-GS	MIN-Avg	FGM-A/%	3PM-A/%	FTM-A/%	OR-DR—TOT/Avg	PF-DQ	A	TO	B	S	PTS/Avg
02-03	6-0	55-9.2	8-12/.667	0-0/.000	3-7/.429	4-5—9/1.5	8-0	6	5	1	1	19/3.2
Total	6-0	55-9.2	8-12/.667	0-0/.000	3-7/.429	4-5—9/1.5	8-0	6	5	1	1	19/3.2

CAREER
Highs

Points *8*
vs. Arkansas-Pine Bluff
(11/27/02)

FG *3*
vs. Arkansas-Pine Bluff
(11/27/02)

FGA *5*
vs. Arkansas-Pine Bluff
(11/27/02)

3P *0*

3PA *0*

FT *2*
vs. Arkansas-Pine Bluff
(11/27/02)

FTA .... *3, twice*
vs. Lehigh (11/24/02) & vs.
Arkansas-Pine Bluff
(11/27/02)

Rebounds .... *3, twice*
vs. Lehigh (11/24/02) & vs.
Eastern Illinois (12/10/02)

Assists *4*
vs. Arkansas-Pine Bluff
(11/27/02)

Blocks *1*
vs. North Carolina (12/3/02)

Steals *1*
vs. Arkansas-Pine Bluff
(11/27/02)

Minutes *18*
vs. Arkansas-Pine Bluff
(11/27/02)

Deron Williams

Sophomore Guard • 6'3" • 210

AT ILLINOIS

2003-2004 Sophomore:
Led the USA Basketball Men's National Junior Team in assists with 38 and was fourth in scoring (8.4 avg.) during the summer while starting all eight games ... Along with teammate Dee Brown, helped the U.S. to a fifth-place finish in Greece with a 7-1 record ... Averaged 13.8 points, 4.7 assists and 4.0 rebounds during Illinois' six-game Scandinavian tour in August.

2002-2003 Freshman: True freshman started 30 of 32 games for the Illini at guard ... Named All-Freshman Team by CollegeInsider.com ... Second on the team and ranked third in the Big Ten in assists, averaging 4.53 per game ... Led the league in assists in conference play with 77 (4.81 apg), edging out teammate Dee Brown by one assist ... Had at least two assists in every game and had five or more assists 16 times ... Ranked second in the Big Ten behind Brown in assist to turnover ratio at +2.46 ... Second on the team with 46 steals, an average of 1.44 spg (ninth in Big Ten) ... Achieved career-high totals in assists (seven) on four occasions, three times in Big Ten play ... Had seven assists and no turnovers vs. Indiana ... Pass-first guard scored in double figures six times during the season ... Scored season-high 12 points three times, including Feb. 18 vs. Michigan State where he hit five of seven shots ... Scored 12 points on four of seven three-point shooting vs. Ohio State ... Excellent defender who usually guarded the opponents' top perimeter player ... Held Indiana's Tom Coverdale to five of 18 shooting and 13 points in the teams' two regular-season meetings ... Held Michigan State sharpshooter Chris Hill to eight points on Feb. 2 and followed that up by holding Ohio State's Brent Darby to six of 21 shooting on Feb. 9 ... One of 12 players on the 2002 USA Basketball Men's Junior World Championship Qualifying Team ... Helped the U.S. to a bronze medal along with fellow Illini Dee Brown.

High School

The Colony, Texas/The Colony H.S.

Consensus Top 50 recruit nationally ... Averaged 17.6 points, 8.4 assists, 6.1 rebounds and 2.6 steals per game as a senior ... Averaged 17 points, 9.4 assists, five rebounds and two steals per game as a junior ... 2001 and 2002 Texas Association of Basketball Coaches (TABC) First-Team All-State selection ... First-team All-State selection by *The Dallas Morning News* ... Helped lead the Cougars to 29-2 mark in 2002 ... Led The Colony to a 32-2 record and the Texas Class 5A state semifinals in 2001 ... Ranked No. 27 in the nation by All-Star Report ... Ranked by RivalsHoops.com as the No. 36 player overall and the No. 8 point guard in the nation ... Ranked No. 46 in the nation by Blue Chip Hoops ... Played in the TABC All-Star game, Kentucky Derby Festival All-Star Classic and Demetrius Johnson St. Louis All-Star game following his senior year ... High school coach was Tommy Thomas.

Personal

Born June 26, 1984, in Parkersburg, W.Va. ... Mother is Denise Smith ... High school teammate of Indiana guard Bracey Wright ... Mother Denise Smith and aunt Judy Ward, played basketball and volleyball at West Liberty State ... Favorite athletes are Jason Kidd ("I love the way he plays the game") and former Illini Frank Williams ... Majoring in sport management.

WILLIAMS'S CAREER STATISTICS

Year	G-GS	MIN-Avg	FGM-A/%	3PM-A/%	FTM-A/%	OR-DR—TOT/Avg	PF-DQ	A	TO	B	S	PTS/Avg
02-03	32-30	868/27.1	75-176/.426	28-79/.354	24-45/.533	15-80—95/3.0	76-2	145	59	5	46	202/6.3
Total	**32-30**	**868/27.1**	**75-176/.426**	**28-79/.354**	**24-45/.533**	**15-80—95/3.0**	**76-2**	**145**	**59**	**5**	**46**	**202/6.3**

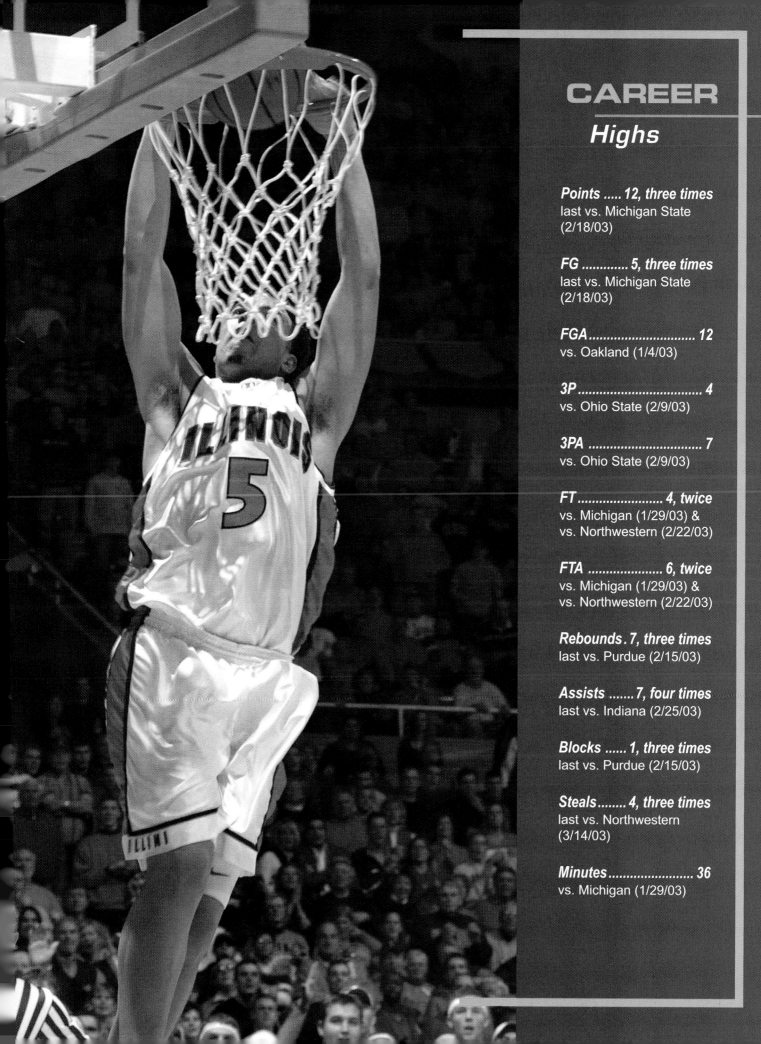

CAREER
Highs

Points ..... *12, three times*
last vs. Michigan State
(2/18/03)

FG .... *5, three times*
last vs. Michigan State
(2/18/03)

FGA 12
vs. Oakland (1/4/03)

3P 4
vs. Ohio State (2/9/03)

3PA 7
vs. Ohio State (2/9/03)

FT .... *4, twice*
vs. Michigan (1/29/03) &
vs. Northwestern (2/22/03)

FTA .... *6, twice*
vs. Michigan (1/29/03) &
vs. Northwestern (2/22/03)

Rebounds. *7, three times*
last vs. Purdue (2/15/03)

Assists .... *7, four times*
last vs. Indiana (2/25/03)

Blocks ...... *1, three times*
last vs. Purdue (2/15/03)

Steals .... *4, three times*
last vs. Northwestern
(3/14/03)

Minutes 36
vs. Michigan (1/29/03)

41

WARREN CARTER

Freshman Forward • 6'9" • 205

High School

Dallas, Texas/Lake Highlands H.S.

Texas Class 5A Player of the Year as a senior ... Texas Association of Basketball Coaches All-State selection ... *Dallas Morning News* All-Area pick ... Played in the THSCA and TABC All-Star games ... Dallas area Defensive Player of the Year ... Averaged 25.6 points, 12.3 rebounds and 5.2 blocks per game as a senior, making 45 three-pointers (37 percent) and shooting 56 percent from the field and 75 percent from the free-throw line ... Totalled 77 steals during his senior season ... Averaged 23.3 points, 10.7 rebounds and 3.5 blocked shots as a junior ... Consensus Top 100 recruit.

Personal

Born April 23, 1985 in Dallas, Texas ... Mother is Kamela Carter ... Has two brothers, Kevin and Joshua ... Enjoys music and volleyball ... Says his biggest thrill in sports will be playing in front of the Orange Krush at the Assembly Hall ... Favorite athlete is NBA player Robert Horry because, "He can do so much and will do anything to help the team win" ... Biggest influence on his athletic career was his high school coach Rob Wiley because he's been a supporting factor since day one of his basketball career ... Brother Kevin plays basketball at Collin County Community College in Texas ... Played AAU ball with the Ft. Worth Lions coached by Mike Hatch, the same team on which future Illini teammate Deron Williams played ... Studying general curriculum as a freshman.

50

JACK INGRAM

Junior Center/Forward • 6'10" • 240

AT ILLINOIS

2003-04 Redshirt Junior:
Will begin the 2003-04 school year with junior eligibility ... Averaged 9.3 points and 5.8 rebounds while shooting 60 percent from the field during Illinois' six-game Scandinavian tour in August.

2002-03 Redshirt Season:
Transferred to Illinois prior to the beginning of the 2002-03 school year and sat out the season per NCAA transfer rules.

At Tulsa

Originally recruited to Tulsa by former UI coach Bill Self ... Lettered two years at Tulsa, playing in 71 games with 11 starts ... Had career averages of 3.7 points and 2.9 rebounds over his two seasons at Tulsa ... Started 11 straight games at one point as a freshman.

High School

San Antonio, Texas/Marshall H.S./Tulsa

Four-year letterwinner at John Marshall High School ... Started both his junior and senior seasons ... Had career averages of 18.0 points and 9.0 rebounds ... Scored at a 22.0 clip and grabbed 11.0 rebounds during his senior season ... Shot 72 percent from the field and 35 percent from three-point range as a senior ... Earned First-Team All-District honors both his junior and senior seasons ... Named to the San Antonio *Express-News* First-Team All-City squad as a senior and to the Second Team his junior season ... High school coach was Terry Morris.

Personal

Born April 23, 1982, in Las Vegas ... Mother is Pam Millisor ... Enjoys fishing, golfing, listening to music, playing video games and reading ... Favorite athlete is Tim Duncan because, "He has no weakness as a player and can beat you in so many different ways with a cool and confident demeanor" ... Majoring in electrical engineering.

RICHARD McBRIDE

Freshman Guard • 6'3" • 210

High School

Springfield, Ill./Lanphier H.S.

Three-time All-State selection by the Champaign *News-Gazette* and Chicago *Sun-Times* and two-time pick by the Associated Press, Illinois Basketball Coaches Association (IBCA) and *Chicago Tribune* ... Finished third in voting for Illinois' Mr. Basketball as a senior ... Four-year letterwinner at Lanphier under Craig Patton, helping the Lions to a 104-23 mark ... Finished his high school career as Lanphier's all-time leading scorer with 2,068 points ... Averaged 24.6 points, 7.9 rebounds and 2.3 assists per game as a senior ... Made 82 three-pointers as a senior ... Earned All-Conference honors all four years of high school ... EA Sports All-American ... Fourth-Team Parade All-American ... Helped Lanphier to second-place finish at 2002 Illinois Class AA state tournament ... Played in the EA Roundball Classic, IBCA and Wendy's Chicago vs. New York All-Star games after his senior season ... Averaged 17 points as a sophomore and was the conference player of the year after helping his team to a 25-4 record ... Averaged 18 points, five rebounds and four assists as a junior while shooting 49 percent from the field and 43 percent from three-point range while helping his team to a 32-2 mark and second place at the state tournament ... Consensus Top 50 recruit ... Played on the 2002 USA Basketball Men's Youth Development Festival.

Personal

Born Jan. 29, 1985 in Springfield, Ill. ... Son of Richard and Bernadine McBride ... Lists his biggest thrill in sports as helping his team to the state tournament as a junior ... Favorite athlete is NBA star Tracy McGrady because of the attitude he shows on and off the court ... Says his parents most influenced his athletics career by sticking by him and pushing him in the right direction ... Studying general curriculum as a freshman.

BRIAN RANDLE

Freshman Forward • 6'8" • 200

High School

Peoria, Ill./Notre Dame H.S.

Three-time All-State selection by the Champaign *News-Gazette* ... Averaged 22.9 points, 12.8 rebounds, 5.2 blocks and 3.1 assists as a senior ... Managed a double-double in 23 of his 26 games ... Finished fourth in voting for Illinois Mr. Basketball as a senior ... First-Team All-State selection by the Chicago *Sun-Times*, Champaign *News-Gazette*, Associated Press and IBCA, and Second-Team by *Chicago Tribune* ... Peoria *Journal-Star* Player of the Year ... High games were 34 points and 22 rebounds ... Had a triple-double by halftime on Jan. 11, 2003 at the Highland Shootout ... Played in the Wendy's Chicago vs. New York All-Star Shootout and IBCA All-Star game following his senior year ... Lettered four times in basketball while in high school .... High school coach was Eddie Matthews ... Consensus Top 50 recruit ... Averaged 16.0 points and 9.8 rebounds as a junior ... Earned Second-Team AP all-state honors as a junior ... AAU teammate with fellow Illini freshman Richard McBride on the Ft. SOOY team coached by Verdell Jones.

Personal

Born Feb. 8, 1985 in Peoria, Ill. ... Parents are Charles and Maryann Randle ... Member of the Notre Dame HS honor roll as a 4.0 student ... National Honor Society member ... HS Student Ambassador... Member of the Liturgy Club while in high school ... Hobbies include cars, cooking and fishing ... Dream in sports is to win a national championship ... Favorite athlete is Grant Hill because of the way he carries himself on and off the court ... Says his father most influenced his athletics career because he didn't push too hard, gave him a base and supported him through all decisions ... Sister Marisa is a junior at the UI ... Studying general curriculum as a freshman.

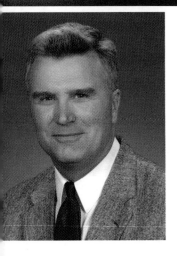

Bruce Weber
Head Coach

A new era of Illinois basketball begins in 2003 as Bruce Weber takes the reins as the 16th Fighting Illini men's basketball coach. After taking the Southern Illinois Salukis to the top of the Missouri Valley Conference with championships each of the last two seasons, he hopes to continue the trend at Illinois where the Illini have won three Big Ten titles in the last six seasons.

Weber, 47, comes to Champaign-Urbana after compiling a 103-54 (.656) record in five seasons as the head coach at Southern Illinois University. He gained 18 years of experience in the Big Ten Conference as an assistant at Purdue under Gene Keady, helping the Boilermakers to six Big Ten championships and 17 postseason appearances.

Energetic and personable, Weber has appeared on numerous national radio and television programs on networks such as ESPN, Fox Sports and CNN. Fame and success have not changed Weber. He remains generous and humble. On road trips, no job is beneath him as he helps team managers load the bus or passes out drinks and sandwiches to his players and staff. Weber's warm personality is likely to make him a popular figure in the state of Illinois as he is a frequent guest at civic clubs, booster club meetings, golf outings and many other speaking engagements.

In his five seasons at SIU, Weber took the Saluki program to the top of the Missouri Valley Conference, winning league titles in 2002 and 2003. He posted records of 28-8 and 24-7 in his last two seasons, leading the Salukis to back-to-back NCAA Tournament appearances including a run to the Sweet Sixteen in 2002 with wins over Texas Tech and Georgia at the United Center in Chicago. Weber's 52 wins over the last two seasons rank among the Top 5 in the nation (only Pittsburgh, Duke, Oklahoma, and Kansas have more victories over that span). His .689 (62-28) winning

percentage in MVC play ranks 12th in the long history of the league. Weber earned Missouri Valley Conference Coach of the Year honors following the 2003 season.

The trademark of the Bruce Weber-led teams at SIU has been aggressive, fundamentally sound defense, holding opponents to 40 percent shooting from the field in 2002 and 2003. On the offensive end, the Salukis averaged 75.5 points in 2002 and 74.5 points last season. He leaves SIU with the Salukis holding a 27-game home-court winning streak.

At the age of 46, Weber has 24 years of coaching experience at the collegiate level with one season at Western Kentucky under Keady before moving with the long-time Boilermaker coach to West Lafayette the following year. He was named the Southern Illinois head coach prior to the 1998-99 season. In his one season at Western Kentucky, the Hilltoppers won the Ohio Valley Conference and advanced to the NCAA Tournament. In his 18 years at Purdue, the Boilermakers won six Big Ten titles, played in 14 NCAA Tournaments and had three NIT appearances.

Weber's association with Keady also allowed Weber to gain experience on the international level. He was an assistant coach for the USA Team at the World University Games in 1989 and head court coach for the Pan American team trials in 1991. Weber assisted Gene Keady in preparation for the Jones Cup, World University Games and Pan American Games.

Born Oct. 19, 1956, the Milwaukee native began his career as a volunteer assistant coach at Madison High School in Milwaukee and a varsity assistant at Marquette University High School.

A 1978 graduate of Wisconsin-Milwaukee, Bruce and his wife, Megan, have three daughters, Hannah (17), Christy (15) and Emily (11).

Personal

Born:
Oct. 19, 1956
in Milwaukee, Wis.

Hometown:
Milwaukee, Wis.

Family:
Wife, Megan; children,
Hannah, Christy and Emily

Education
High School:
Milwaukee Marshall
High School (1974)

College:
University of Wisconsin-
Milwaukee
(bachelor's in education, 1978)

Coaching Experience

1979-80—Western Kentucky University
Assistant coach at Western Kentucky under Gene Keady, helping the
Hilltoppers to a 21-8 record and an NCAA Tournament appearance.

1980-98—Purdue University
Followed Gene Keady and served as assistant coach for 18 years.
• Purdue had an overall 415-176 record during that time span.
• During his 18-year stint, Purdue advanced to postseason play 17
   times, including 14 times to the NCAA Tournament and three appear-
   ances in the NIT.
• The Boilers won six Big Ten titles during his 18 seasons.

1998-2003—Southern Illinois University
Appointed head coach at Southern Illinois University in April, 1998
• Registered an overall coaching record of 103-54 in five seasons, but
over the last two seasons compiled a 52-15 mark • Led SIU to Missouri
Valley Conference titles in 2002 and 2003 • Took the Salukis to the 2002
NCAA Sweet 16 with a 28-8 mark • Earned MVC Coach of the Year
honors after winning second conference title with 24-7 record in 2003
•Took SIU to the NIT in 2000 with a 20-13 mark • Finished his SIU career
with a 62-28 record in MVC play, the 12th-best winning percentage (.689)
in conference history.

2003-04—University of Illinois
Named Illinois' 16th head coach on April 30, 2003.

CAREER COACHING RECORD

ASSISTANT COACH

Western Kentucky University, head coach Gene Keady

	Overall Record	Postseason Play
1979-80	21-8 (.724)	NCAA

Purdue University, head coach Gene Keady (1981-98)

1980-81	21-11 (.656)	NIT Final Four
1981-82	18-14 (.563)	NIT Runnerup
1982-83	21-9 (.700)	NCAA
1983-84	22-7 (.759)	NCAA, Big Ten Champs
1984-85	20-9 (.690)	NCAA
1985-86	22-10 (.688)	NCAA
1986-87	25-5 (.833)	NCAA, Big Ten Champs
1987-88	29-4 (.879)	NCAA, Sweet 16, Big Ten Champs
1988-89	15-16 (.484)	
1989-90	22-8 (.733)	NCAA
1990-91	17-12 (.586)	NCAA
1991-92	18-15 (.545)	NIT
1992-93	18-10 (.643)	NCAA
1993-94	29-5 (853)	NCAA, Big Ten Champs
1994-95	25-7 (.781)	NCAA, Big Ten Champs
1995-96	26-6 (.813)	NCAA, Big Ten Champs
1996-97	18-12 (.600)	NCAA
1997-98	28-8 (.778)	NCAA, Sweet 16

HEAD COACH

Southern Illinois University

1998-99	15-12 (.556)	
1999-2000	20-13 (.606)	NIT
2000-01	16-14 (533)	
2001-02	28-8 (.778)	
NCAA,		
Sweet 16,		
MVC Champs		
2002-03	24-7 (.774)	
NCAA,		
MVC Champs		

Five Years	103-54 (.656)	
MVC Record	62-28 (.689)	

NCAA Tournament Record: 2-2 (.500)

CHRIS LOWERY

Assistant Coach

"Chris has plenty of experience, having played four years at SIU and then working his way up in the coaching profession the past eight years. I'm thrilled to have Chris join the staff here at Illinois."

—Bruce Weber

CHRIS LOWERY begins his first season as an assistant coach with the Fighting Illini after being named to the staff on May 7, 2003. Lowery arrives at Illinois after serving as an assistant under Weber at Southern Illinois the past two seasons.

The Evansville, Ind., native was a four-year letterwinner at Southern Illinois, helping lead the team to two straight NCAA Tournament appearances in 1993 and '94 after consecutive NIT berths in 1991 and '92. The three-year starting point guard was a Second-Team All-Missouri Valley selection in 1992. Lowery scored 1,225 career points and dished out 391 assists, ranking third in school history on the career assists chart. SIU went 86-37 (.699) during his four years.

Lowery was an assistant coach at Missouri Southern State College for three years, helping the Lions to a 30-3 record and an NCAA Division II Final Four appearance in 2000.

Prior to his coaching tenure at Southern Illinois, Lowery spent one season as an assistant at Southeast Missouri State under Gary Garner.

"Chris worked very hard the past two years as an assistant at Southern Illinois," Weber said. "He does a great job with recruiting and has a good relationship with the players."

Lowery, 30, graduated from Southern Illinois in 1996 with a bachelor's degree in physical education. He and his wife, Erika, have three children, Lexis, C.J. and Kahari.

PERSONAL

Hometown:
Evansville, Ind.

Family:
Wife, Erika; children,
Lexis, C.J. and Kahari

Education:
Southern Illinois (bachelor's,1996)

Coaching Experience:
1996-97
Assistant Coach
Rend Lake Community College

1998-2000
Assistant Coach
Missouri Southern State College

2000-01
Assistant Coach
Southeast Missouri State University

2001-03
Assistant Coach
Southern Illinois University

2003-04
Assistant Coach
University of Illinois

LOWERY FILE

WAYNE McCLAIN
Assistant Coach

"Wayne gives us continuity in the program, plus is a person who is known and respected throughout the state of Illinois because of his program at Manual. Add to the fact that both his son and daughter attended the university, and it shows he has great pride in Illinois."

—Bruce Weber

McCLAIN FILE

PERSONAL

Hometown:
Peoria, Ill.

Family:
Wife, Robin; Children, Sergio and Brindeshie

Education:
Bradley University (bachelor's, 1977)
Illinois State University (master's, 1982)

Coaching Experience:
1978-94
Assistant Coach
Peoria (Ill.) Manual High School

1995-2001
Head Coach
Peoria (Ill.) Manual High School

2001-04
Assistant Coach
University of Illinois

WAYNE McCLAIN begins his third year with the Fighting Illini coaching staff after a legendary prep career at Peoria Manual High School. He came to Illinois following an illustrious seven-year career as head coach at Manual where he led the Rams to three-straight AA state championships in his first three years as coach. *USA Today* named his 1997 squad, led by future Illini Sergio McClain (his son), Marcus Griffin and Frank Williams, National High School Champions, and the senior McClain was named National High School Coach of the Year.

The Rams had records of 32-2, 31-2 and 31-1 in his first three seasons as head coach, winning state titles each season. McClain also earned Illinois Basketball Coaches Association Coach of the Year in 1995, '96 and '97.

He began his high school career in 1978, serving as an assistant basketball coach to the legendary Dick Van Scyoc for 18 years until being named head coach in 1995. While at Manual, McClain coached four future Illini players including Jerry Hester, Marcus Griffin, Sergio McClain, and Frank Williams.

McClain lettered for the Bradley basketball team in 1975. He earned a master's degree in physical education at Illinois State University in 1982 while teaching at Manual.

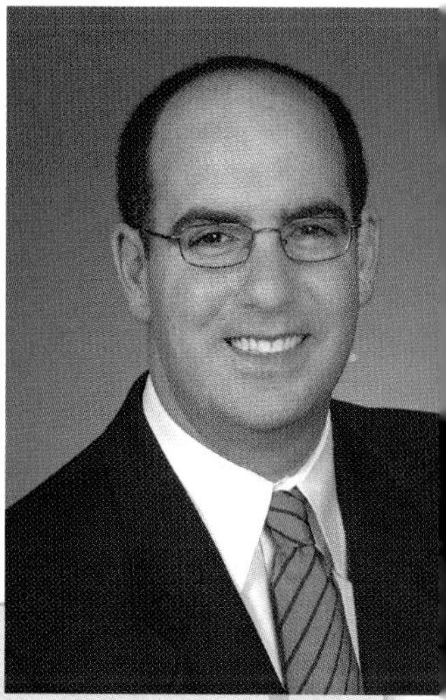

"Jay is one of the most experienced coaches in the Big Ten and knows what it takes to be successful in our conference."

—Bruce Weber

JAY PRICE begins his first season at Illinois after he joined the Fighting Illini basketball staff on May 14, 2003.

Price comes to Illinois after spending the past 10 years as an assistant coach at Purdue under Gene Keady. In addition to his normal coaching and scouting duties, Price served as Purdue's recruiting coordinator and oversaw summer basketball camps, team travel and scheduling. During his time at Purdue, the Boilermakers compiled a record of 220-105 (.677), winning three Big Ten championships and earning eight NCAA Tournament berths. Weber and Price worked together as assistants on the Purdue staff for five seasons, from 1994-98.

"I'm extremely excited to have Jay Price join our staff and look forward to working with him again," Weber said. "Jay is a very hard worker who will prove to be quite an asset at Illinois."

Price began his coaching career with a two-year stint as an assistant at Oklahoma under former coach Billy Tubbs before going to Purdue. During that time, he also served as manager for the U.S. Olympic men's basketball "Dream Team" while the squad practiced in the United States during the summer of 1992.

A native of Oklahoma City, Okla., Price was a basketball manager at Kansas for four years under former coaches Larry Brown and Roy Williams, serving as head manager for Williams as both a junior and senior. During his time at Kansas, the Jayhawks won the national championship in 1988 and finished as national runner-up in 1991.

Price is the vice president of the NABC assistant coaches' committee.

Price, 34, received a bachelor's degree in journalism from Kansas in 1991.

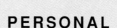

PERSONAL

Hometown:
Oklahoma City, Okla.

Family:
Wife, Beth; daughter, Katherine

Education:
University of Kansas (bachelor's, 1991)

Coaching Experience:
1992-94
Assistant Coach
University of Oklahoma

1994-2003
Assistant Coach
Purdue University

2003-04
Assistant Coach
University of Illinois

PRICE FILE

Kenny Battle is, quite possibly, the most popular player in Illini history. The loveable lefty was the leader of the "Flyin' Illini" team that earned a spot in the Final Four in Seattle in March of '89. Battle went on to a 10-year professional career that included five seasons in the NBA with Denver, Golden State, Boston, and Phoenix. He also played in the CBA, where he was a part of a championship team with the LaCrosse Catbirds. After a season as an assistant coach with the Harlem Globetrotters, Battle is gearing up for his first year as a college head coach. Battle is married with five children and another due in December.

What are you doing these days?

I'm the head coach at Illinois Institute of Technology in southern Chicago. I'm really excited about it. We'll win and lose with class, and we'll be exciting to watch.

What's your greatest memory of your time spent at UI?

The greatest would have to be the Final Four. That team was so close. And we just willed ourselves not to lose—most of the time. I think about that loss to Michigan every day. I know Kendall [Gill] told someone he hasn't watched the game yet. You always wonder "What if?" "What could I have done differently?" It's very special to know that that year everyone in the country and around the world knew about Illinois basketball. They knew about a team that was undersized and exciting to watch. I get people still to this day talking about that team. It's something to remember.

Which of your former teammates do you stay in touch with?

I spoke to three in the last week. Marcus [Liberty]. Lowell [Hamilton]. And I talked to Larry Smith. [Stephen] Bardo's busy, but I spoke to him when I interviewed here [at IIT].

What do you miss most about Champaign-Urbana?

I miss the community. Those three years I was there, the community deeply and truly was there for the team. They reached out to us and embraced us and said, "Hey, we're here to support you guys." And they did. Bunches of people deeply care about Illinois basketball. That's something you always miss. We represented the entire state and I think we did a good job doing it.

What's it like to have an award named for you?

I was very honored. Most awards are named after you once you're dead. Fortunately I was able to see it. I think it showed what Coach Henson thought I brought to the game. I was given a talent and given it for a reason—to excite fans and inspire young men I come in contact with.

Who's your favorite current Illini?

I would have to say Dee Brown because of the excitement he brings, the emotion he shows, and his willingness to do everything he can do. For his size, he's remarkable. He'll do whatever it takes. He's that individual you can count on.

Have you met Coach Weber?

I've talked to Coach Weber. He sent me a congrats card. I don't know him [well], but others tell me he's a great choice. He'll represent the school very well and be dedicated to Illinois basketball. And all those qualities will mean success for the program there.

Former Illini great Stephen Bardo (left) and Brian Barnhart team up for Fighting Illini basketball broadcasts on the Illini Sports Network.

ILLINI SPORTS NETWORK

Aledo, WRMJ-FM 102.3
Alton, WBGZ-AM 1570
Bloomington, WJEZ-FM 93.7
Carterville, WJPF-AM 1340
Carterville, WCIL-AM 1020
Casey, WCBH-FM 104.3
Champaign, WDWS-AM 1400
Champaign, WHMS-FM 97.5
Chicago, WSCR-AM 670
Danville, WDAN-AM 1490
Danville, WDNL-FM, 102.1
Davenport, Iowa, WLLR-AM 1230
Decatur, WSOY-AM 1340
DuQuoin, WDQN-AM 1580
Effingham, WCRC-FM 95.7
Fairfield, WFIW-AM 1390
Galesburg, WGIL-AM 1400
Highland, WCBW-AM 880
Jacksonville, WJIL-AM 1550
Kankakee, WKAN-AM 1320
Kewanee, WYEC-FM 93.9
Litchfield, WSMI-FM 106.1
Mt. Carmel, WVMC-AM 1360
Mattoon, WCRC-FM 95.7
Newton, WIKK-FM 103.5
Olney, WVLN-AM 740
Olney, WSEI-FM 92.9
Paris, WPRS-AM 1440
Paris, WACF-FM 98.5
Paxton, WPXN-FM 104.9
Peoria, WWFS-AM 1290
Pontiac, WJEZ-FM 93.7
Quincy, WTAD-AM 930
Robinson, WTAY-AM 1570
Robinson, WTYE-FM 101.7
Rockford, WROK-AM 1440
Rock Island, WKBF-AM 1270
Salem, WJBD-AM 1350
Salem, WJBD-FM 100.1
Sparta, WHCO-AM 1230
St. Louis, KRFT-AM 1190
Springfield, WTAX-AM 1240
Taylorville, WTIM-FM 97.3
Vandalia, WPMB-AM 1500
Watseka, WGFA-FM 94.1

The 45-station Illini Sports Network once again will bring Fighting Illini basketball to fans across the state with Brian Barnhart and former Illini great Stephen Bardo calling the action from courtside.

Barnhart is in his second season as the "Voice of the Illini" after a long stint in professional baseball, including two years as the play-by-play voice of the Anaheim Angels. Barnhart serves as the voice of the Illini Sports Network, providing play-by-play coverage of football and men's basketball, and as the host of the statewide "Ron Turner Show" and "Bruce Weber Show" call-in programs every Monday night at 6:05 p.m. "Bruce Weber Live" can be heard on Monday nights from 6-7 p.m. beginning Dec. 8.

A native of nearby Tolono, Barnhart graduated from Unity High School and Liberty University before beginning a 15-year career in professional baseball as a play-by-play announcer in 1986.

In 1998, Barnhart was named the play-by-play announcer for the Angels and spent two full seasons with the American League club before returning to the Champaign-Urbana area in 2000. He currently is a news and sports announcer at WDWS-AM 1400 in Champaign.

Former Illini star guard Stephen Bardo will be in his fourth season as an expert analyst for the Illini Sports Network. A 1990 graduate of the UI, Bardo was a mainstay on the Flying Illini team that reached the Final Four in 1989. A hard-nosed defensive specialist, Bardo went on to a nine-year professional career that included stops in the NBA, CBA, USBL, Italy, Spain, France, Venezuela and most recently Japan. He has broadcasting experience working with ESPN-Plus Regional, CLTV in Chicago and on ESPN International NBA broadcasts. He is currently a sports reporter at WBBM-TV in Chicago.

2003-04 Fighting Illini Season Schedule

DAY	DATE	OPPONENT	LOCATION	TV	TIME
Sat	11/01/2003	ORANGE & BLUE SCRIMMAGE	ASSEMBLY HALL		7 p.m.
Sun	11/09/2003	ILLINOIS ALL-STARS (Exh.)	ASSEMBLY HALL		4 p.m.
Mon	11/17/2003	SPOTLIGHT JAMMERS (Exh.)	ASSEMBLY HALL		7 p.m.
Sat	11/22/2003	WESTERN ILLINOIS	ASSEMBLY HALL		7 p.m.
Wed	11/26/2003	MERCER	ASSEMBLY HALL		7 p.m.
Sat	11/29/2003	Temple	Philadelphia, Pa.	ESPN2	3 p.m.
Tue	12/02/2003	North Carolina	Greensboro, N.C.	ESPN	8 p.m.
Sat	12/06/2003	Arkansas	Chicago, Ill.	ESPN+ Local	11 a.m.
Tue	12/09/2003	Providence	New York, N.Y.	ESPN	6 p.m.
Thu	12/11/2003	MARYLAND-EASTERN SHORE	ASSEMBLY HALL		7 p.m.
Sat	12/13/2003	MEMPHIS	ASSEMBLY HALL	ESPN2	8 p.m.
Tue	12/23/2003	Missouri	St. Louis, Mo.	ESPN2	8 p.m.
Tue	12/30/2003	Illinois-Chicago	Chicago, Ill.		7 p.m.
Sat	01/03/2004	ILLINOIS STATE	ASSEMBLY HALL	ESPN+ Local	1 p.m.
Wed	01/07/2004	OHIO STATE	ASSEMBLY HALL	ESPN+ Local	8 p.m.
Sat	01/10/2004	PURDUE	ASSEMBLY HALL	ESPN+ Regional	3:30 p.m.
Wed	01/14/2004	Northwestern	Evanston, Ill.	ESPN+ Local	7 p.m.
Sat	01/17/2004	IOWA	ASSEMBLY HALL	ESPN	11 a.m.
Wed	01/21/2004	PENN STATE	ASSEMBLY HALL	ESPN+ Local	8 p.m.
Sat	01/24/2004	Wisconsin	Madison, Wis.	ESPN+ Regional	1:30 p.m.
Sat	01/31/2004	MICHIGAN	ASSEMBLY HALL	CBS	12:45 p.m.
Tue	02/03/2004	Indiana	Bloomington, Ind.	ESPN	6 p.m.
Sun	02/08/2004	Minnesota	Minneapolis, Minn.	CBS	Noon
Tue	02/10/2004	MICHIGAN STATE	ASSEMBLY HALL	ESPN	8 p.m.
Wed	02/18/2004	WISCONSIN	ASSEMBLY HALL	ESPN+ Local	7 p.m.

DAY	DATE	OPPONENT	LOCATION	TV	TIME
Sat	02/21/2004	Penn State	University Park, Pa.	ESPN	3 p.m.
Wed	02/25/2004	Iowa	Iowa City, Iowa	ESPN+ Local	6 p.m.
Sat	02/28/2004	NORTHWESTERN	ASSEMBLY HALL	ESPN+ Regional	1:30 p.m.
Tue	03/02/2004	Purdue	West Lafayette, Ind.	ESPN	6 p.m.
	-or-				
Wed	03/03/2004	Purdue	West Lafayette, Ind.	ESPN+ Local	TBA
Sat	03/06/2004	Ohio State	Columbus, Ohio	ESPN+ Regional	11:15 a.m.
	-or-				
Sun	03/07/2004	Ohio State	Columbus, Ohio	CBS	3 p.m.
Thu	03/11/2004	Big Ten Tournament - Opening Round	Indianapolis, Ind.	TBA	TBA
Fri	03/12/2004	Big Ten Tournament Quarterfinals	Indianapolis, Ind.	TBA	TBA
Sat	03/13/2004	Big Ten Tournament Semifinals	Indianapolis, Ind.	CBS	TBA
Sun	03/14/2004	Big Ten Tournament Championship	Indianapolis, Ind.	CBS	TBA
Thu	03/18/2004	NCAA Tournament - First Round	TBA	CBS	TBA
Fri	03/19/2004	NCAA Tournament - First Round	TBA	CBS	TBA
Sat	03/20/2004	NCAA Tournament - Second Round	TBA	CBS	TBA
Sun	03/21/2004	NCAA Tournament - Second Round	TBA	CBS	TBA
Thu	03/25/2004	NCAA Regional Semifinals	TBA	CBS	TBA
Fri	03/26/2004	NCAA Regional Semifinals	TBA	CBS	TBA
Sat	03/27/2004	NCAA Regional Finals	TBA	CBS	TBA
Sun	03/28/2004	NCAA Regional Finals	TBA	CBS	TBA
Sat	04/03/2004	NCAA Final Four	San Antonio, Texas	CBS	TBA
Mon	04/05/2004	NCAA National Championship	San Antonio, Texas	CBS	TBA

Dates and times subject to change.

Television coverage subject to change.

All times are Central.

Arkansas

Saturday, Dec. 6, 2003 at Chicago, Ill., 11 a.m. ESPN+ Local

Quick Facts

Location: Fayetteville, Ark.

Enrollment: 16,035

Nickname: Razorbacks

Conference: Southeastern (Western Division)

Head Coach: Stan Heath

Collegiate Coaching Record: 39-25 (2 years)

Record at Arkansas: 9-19 (1 year)

Assistant Coaches: Ronny Thompson, Rob Flaska and Oronde Taliaferro

2002-03 Overall Record: 9-19

2002-03 Conference Record/ Finish: 4-12/5th in West

Starters Returning/Lost: 2/3

Letterman Returning/Lost: 8/5

Website: www.hogwired.com

2003-04 Arkansas Razorbacks Roster

Player	Ht.	Wt.	Yr.	Pos.	Hometown	ppg/rpg/apg
Jamar Blackmon	6-3	195	Sr.	G	Little Rock, Ark.	0.7/0.4/0.3
Ronnie Brewer	6-6	190	Fr.	G	Fayetteville, Ark.	
Preston Cranford	6-7	185	Fr.	G	Heber Springs, Ark.	
Kendrick Davis	6-3	171	So.	G	Houston, Texas	10.3/2.0/1.4
Olu Famutimi	6-5	210	Fr.	G/F	Flint, Mich.	
Eric Ferguson	6-1	196	So.	PG	Long Island, N.Y.	10.9/3.1/3.2
Vincent Hunter	6-9	195	Fr.	F	Little Rock, Ark.	
Michael Jones	6-9	220	Jr.	F	Little Rock, Ark.	5.3/2.5/0.4
Jonathon Modica	6-4	198	So.	G/F	Smackover, Ark.	11.5/4.5/0.6
Wenbos Mukubu	6-5	197	So.	G/F	Van Buren, Ark.	
Rashard Sullivan	6-8	221	So.	F	Ft. Lauderdale, Fla.	2.4/3.2/0.4
Charles Tatum	5-10	166	Sr.	G	Midland, Texas	

Series History

Series: Illinois leads 3-0
Games at Illinois: Illinois leads 1-0
Games at Arkansas: N/A
Neutral Games: Illinois leads 2-0
Last Illinois Win: 62-58 (12/7/02, Little Rock)
Last Arkansas Win: N/A
Longest Illinois win streak: 3 Current
Longest Illinois home win streak: 1 (1949) Current
Longest Illinois away win streak: N/A

Longest Arkansas win streak: N/A
Longest Arkansas home win streak: N/A
Longest Arkansas away win streak: N/A
Current Series Streak: Illinois W-3
Illinois' Largest Winning Margin: 12 (65-53), Dec. 14, 1949, at Champaign
Arkansas' Largest Winning Margin: N/A
Weber vs. Arkansas: 0-0
Heath vs. Illinois at Arkansas: 0-1

Quick Facts

Location: Bloomington, Ill.

Enrollment: 21,035

Nickname: Redbirds

Conference: Missouri Valley

Head Coach: Porter Moser

Collegiate Record: 54-34 (4 years)

Record at Illinois State: First season

Assistant Coaches: Brian Barone, Steve Forbes, Daniyal Robinson

2002-03 Record: 8-21

2002-03 Conference Record (Finish): 5-13/9th

Starters Returning/Lost: 3/2

Lettermen Returning/Lost: 7/3

Website: www.redbirds.org

2003-04 Illinois State Redbirds Roster

Player	Ht.	Wt.	Yr.	Pos.	Hometown	ppg/rpg/apg
Gregg Alexander	6-4	195	Jr.	G/F	Lincoln, Ill.	11.1/3.0/1.3
Marcus Arnold	6-7	225	So.	F	Chicago, Ill.	8.4/3.4/0.4
Chris Burras	6-5	210	So.	F	Chicago, Ill.	2.8/2.8/0.5
Ronnie Carlwell	6-10	250	Fr.	C	Maywood, Ill.	
Greg Dilligard	6-8	215	Fr.	F	Labelle, Mo.	
Najeeb Echols	6-7	230	Jr.	F	Chicago, Ill.	
Dana Ford	6-4	185	So.	G	Tamms, Ill.	2.0/2.5/0.6
Vince Greene	5-9	160	Sr.	G	Chicago, Ill.	12.3/2.7/4.4
Trey Guidry	6-2	185	Jr.	G	Baton Rouge, La.	11.1/1.6/1.5
Rebert Harris	6-0	177	Sr.	G	Chicago, Ill.	0.4/0.3/0.1
Kenneth Hill	6-6	190	So.	F	Naperville, Ill.	1.6/0.5/0.0
Neil Plank	6-5	200	Jr.	G/F	Mt. Zion, Ill.	
Michael Sams	6-7	215	Fr.	F	Decatur, Ill.	
Kevin Troc	6-4	190	So.	G	Lockport, Ill.	2.2/1.2/0.8

Series History

Series: Illinois leads 6-0
Games at Illinois: Illinois leads 5-0
Games at Illinois State: Illinois leads 1-0
Neutral Site: N/A
Last Illinois win: 87-73 (12/18/01, Champaign)
Last Illinois State win: N/A
Longest Illinois winning streak: 6 (current)
Longest Illinois home winning streak: 5, (1921-2001) Current
Longest Illinois road winning streak: 1, (1920) Current

Longest ISU winning streak: N/A
Longest ISU home winning streak: N/A
Longest ISU road winning streak: N/A
Current Series Streak: Illinois W-6, Current
Illinois Largest Winning Margin: 25 (42-17), Jan. 10, 1921, at Champaign
ISU's Largest Winning Margin: N/A
Weber vs. Illinois State all-time: 8-3
Moser vs. Illinois at Illinois State: First Meeting

Illinois-Chicago

Quick Facts

Location: Chicago, Ill.

Enrollment: 24,541

Nickname: Flames

Conference: Horizon League

Head Coach: Jimmy Collins

Collegiate Record: 107-101 (7 years)

Record at UIC: Same

Assistant Coaches: Mark Coomes, Lynn Mitchem, Dave Donnelly

2002-03 Record: 21-9

2002-03 Conference Record (Finish): 12-4/3rd

Starters Returning/Lost: 5/0

Lettermen Returning/Lost: 8/2

Website: www.uicflames.com

2003-04 Illinois-Chicago Flames Roster

Player	Ht.	Wt.	Yr.	Pos.	Hometown	ppg/rpg/apg
Mike Smith	6-2	170	So.	G	Calumet Park, Ill.	1.0/0.6/0.2
Martell Bailey	5-10	170	Sr.	G	Chicago, Ill.	10.0/3.7/8.1
Jovan Stefanov	6-9	210	Fr.	G	Belgrade, Yugoslavia	
Richard Lesko	6-9	210	Sr.	F	Kosice, Slovakia	2.5/1.6/0.2
Marcetteaus McGee	6-1	160	Fr.	G	Chicago, Ill.	
Rickey Dominguez	6-4	190	Sr.	G	Aurora, Ill.	1.3/1.3/0.3
Justin Bowen	6-6	190	So.	F	Chicago, Ill.	
Armond Williams	6-4	205	Sr.	F	Hillside, Ill.	13.6/7.6/1.0
Aaron Carr	6-4	195	Sr.	F	Chicago, Ill.	11.3/4.2/2.2
Cedrick Banks	6-2	165	Sr.	G	Chicago, Ill.	19.0/5.0/1.9
Jabari Harris	6-9	215	Sr.	F/C	Broadview, Ill.	1.6/1.4/0.1
Kevin Mitchem	6-6	190	Sr.	F	Grandview, Mo.	0.8/1.4/0.0
Joe Scott	6-9	215	Sr.	F	Palos Hills, Ill.	4.8/3.0/0.2
Josh Williams	6-8	220	So.	F	Chicago, Ill.	1.2/1.2/0.2
Elliott Poole	6-7	255	So.	F	Chicago, Ill.	
Josip Petrusic	6-10	240	Jr.	C	Zagreb, Croatia	
Brandon Allen	6-9	240	So.	F	Chicago, Ill.	

Series History

Series: Illinois leads 10-1

Games at Illinois: Illinois leads 7-1

Games at UIC: Illinois leads 1-0

Neutral Site Games: Illinois leads 2-0

Last Illinois win: 77-64 (12/21/01, Rosemont)

Last UIC win: 60-71 (11/29/90, Champaign)

Longest Illinois winning streak: 8 (Current)

Longest Illinois home winning streak: 5 (1992-1997) Current

Longest Illinois road winning streak: 2 (1991-1996) Current

Longest UIC winning streak: 1 (1990)

Longest UIC home winning streak: N/A

Longest UIC road winning streak: 1 (1990)

Current Series Streak: Illinois W-8

Illinois Largest Winning Margin: 56 (109-53) Dec. 11, 1987, at Champaign

UIC Largest Winning Margin: 11 (71-60) Nov. 29, 1990 at Champaign

Weber vs. UIC all-time: 3-2

Colllins vs. Illinois at UIC: 0-3

Indiana

Quick Facts

Location: Bloomington, Ind.

Enrollment: 36,000

Nickname: Hoosiers

Conference: Big Ten

Head Coach: Mike Davis

Collegiate Record: 67-38 (3 years)

Record at Indiana: Same

Assistant Coaches: John Treloar, Ben McDonald, Thad Fitzpatrick

2002-03 Record: 21-13

2002-03 Conference Record (Finish): 8-8/6th

Starters Returning/Lost: 3/2

Lettermen Returning/Lost: 9/3

Website: www.iuhoosiers.com

2003-04 schedule

Nov. 21 UNC-Greensboro
Nov. 24 at Vanderbilt
Nov. 29 vs. Xavier
Dec. 2 at Wake Forest
Dec. 6 Missouri
Dec. 10 at Notre Dame
Dec. 13 Butler
Dec. 20 vs. Kentucky
Dec. 23 Morehead State
Dec. 29 at North Texas
Jan. 3 Temple
Jan. 6 at Wisconsin
Jan. 11 at Michigan
Jan. 17 Northwestern
Jan. 20 at Ohio State
Jan. 24 at Minnesota
Jan. 27 Purdue
Jan. 31 at Michigan State
Feb. 3 Illinois
Feb. 7 Iowa
Feb. 11 at Penn State
Feb. 14 at Purdue
Feb. 18 Minnesota
Feb. 21 Ohio State
Feb. 25 at Northwestern
Mar. 2 or 3 Michigan
Mar. 6 or 7 Wisconsin
Mar. 11-14 Big Ten Tournament

2003-04 Indiana Hoosiers Roster

Player	Ht.	Wt.	Yr.	Pos.	Hometown	ppg/rpg/apg
Pat Ewing Jr.	6-8	215	Fr.	F	Ft. Washington, Md.	
Jessan Gray-Ashley	6-10	190	Fr.	F	Davenport, Iowa	
Mark Johnson	6-2	190	Jr.	G	Oregon, Wis.	
Sean Kline	6-8	235	Jr.	F	Huntington, Ind.	2.8/1.9/0.4
George Leach	6-11	240	Sr.	C	Charlotte, N.C.	6.5/5.5/0.4
A.J. Moye	6-3	215	Sr.	G	Atlanta, Ga.	5.5/3.9/0.8
Donald Perry	6-2	185	Jr.	G	Tallulah, La.	2.2/0.8/0.4
Mike Roberts	6-9	220	Sr.	F	Eugene, Ore.	1.4/1.3/0.1
Jason Stewart	6-8	235	Sr.	F	Edwardsport, Ind.	
Marshall Strickland	6-2	195	So.	G	Winfield, Md.	6.1/2.4/2.0
Ryan Tapak	6-2	180	Jr.	G	Indianapolis, Ind.	
Roderick Wilmont	6-4	195	So.	G	Miramar, Fla.	
Bracey Wright	6-3	185	So.	G	The Colony, Texas	16.2/5.0/2.1

Series History

Series: Indiana leads 78-72
Games at Illinois: Illinois leads 43-30
Games at Indiana: Indiana leads 47-26
Neutral Games: Illinois leads 3-1
Last Illinois Win: 73-72 (3/15/03, at Chicago)
Last Indiana Win: 74-66 (1/18/03, at Bloomington)
Longest Illinois win streak: 8 (1912-1923)
Longest Illinois home win streak: 11 (1906-1925)
Longest Illinois away win streak: 3 (three times, last 1988-1990)

Longest Indiana win streak: 9 (1972-1977)
Longest Indiana home win streak: 6 (1991-96)
Longest Indiana away win streak: 5 (1971-76)
Current Series Streak: Illinois W-2
Illinois' Largest Winning Margin: 29 (35-6), Jan. 6, 1914 at Urbana
Indiana's Largest Winning Margin: 40 (107-67), Feb. 9, 1974 at Bloomington
Weber vs. Indiana all-time: 1-0
Davis vs. Illinois at Indiana: 3-4

Iowa

Saturday, Jan. 17, 2004 at Champaign, Ill. 11 a.m. ESPN
Wednesday, Feb. 5, 2004 at Iowa City, Iowa, 6 p.m. ESPN+ Local

2003-04 schedule

Nov. 23 UNC-Asheville
Nov. 25 Drake
Nov. 29 Louisville
Dec. 2 Wisconsin-Green Bay
Dec. 5 Eastern Washington
Dec. 9 at Northern Iowa
Dec. 22 Texas Tech
Dec. 30 Eastern Illinois
Jan. 3 at Missouri
Jan. 7 Purdue
Jan. 10 Northwestern
Jan. 13 at Minnesota
Jan. 17 at Illinois
Jan. 21 at Iowa State
Jan. 24 Ohio State
Jan. 28 at Michigan
Jan. 31 Penn State
Feb. 4 at Michigan State
Feb. 7 at Indiana
Feb. 11 Wisconsin
Feb. 14 Michigan
Feb. 18 at Ohio State
Feb. 25 Illinois
Feb. 28 Minnesota
Mar. 3 at Northwestern
Mar. 6 at Purdue
Mar. 11-14 Big Ten Tournament

Quick Facts

Location: Iowa City, Iowa
Enrollment: 28,311
Nickname: Hawkeyes
Conference: Big Ten
Head Coach: Steve Alford
Collegiate Record: 229-135 (12 years)
Record at Iowa: 73-58 (Four years)

Assistant Coaches: Brian Jones, Greg Lansing, Rich Walker
2002-03 Record: 17-14
2002-03 Conference Record (Finish): 7-8/T-8th
Starters Returning/Lost: 4/1
Lettermen Returning/Lost: 8/4
Website: www.hawkeyesports.com

2003-04 Iowa Hawkeyes roster

Player	Ht.	Wt.	Yr.	Pos.	Hometown	ppg/rpg/apg
Brody Boyd	5-11	165	Sr.	G	Dugger, Ind.	9.7/2.1/1.4
Jack Brownlee	6-0	165	Jr.	G	Ft. Dodge, Iowa	
Greg Brunner	6-7	240	So.	F	Charles City, Iowa	7.5/5.2/1.5
Nick Dewitz	6-8	215	So.	F	Chandler, Ariz.	
Adam Haluska	6-5	210	So.	G	Carroll, Iowa	
Erek Hansen	6-11	210	So.	C	Bedford, Texas	
Mike Henderson	6-2	190	Fr.	G	Waterloo, Iowa	
Jeff Horner	6-3	185	So.	G	Mason City, Iowa	8.2/4.4/4.5
Pierre Pierce	6-4	195	So.	G	Westmont, Ill.	
Ben Rand	6-6	185	Fr.	G	Rochelle, Ill.	
Jared Reiner	6-11	255	Sr.	C	Tripp, S.D.	9.7/8.3/1.4
Sean Sonderleiter	6-9	235	Sr.	C	Des Moines, Iowa	8.5/4.0/1.0
Kurt Spurgeon	6-5	195	Sr.	F	DeWitt, Iowa	1.0/0.8/0.1
Glen Worley	6-7	218	Sr.	F	Coralville, Iowa	10.9/5.2/1.5

Series History

Series: Illinois leads 68-64
Games at Illinois: Illinois leads 53-14
Games at Iowa: Iowa leads 49-16
Neutral Games: N/A
Last Illinois Win: 77-66 (1/15/02, at Champaign)
Last Iowa Win: 68-61 (1/15/03, at Iowa City)
Longest Illinois win streak: 5 (1963-1965)
Longest Illinois home win streak: 15 (1931-1951)
Longest Illinois away win streak: 3 (1962-1964)
Longest Iowa win streak: 6 (1975-1977)

Longest Iowa home win streak: 10 (1965-1977)
Longest Iowa away win streak: 3 (1975-1977)
Current Series Streak: Iowa W-1
Illinois' Largest Winning Margin: 32 (66-34), Jan. 19, 1943 at Champaign
Iowa's Largest Winning Margin: 25 (95-70), Jan. 4, 1975 at Iowa City
Weber vs. Iowa all-time: First Meeting
Alford vs. Illinois at Iowa: 2-4

Maryland-Eastern Shore

Quick Facts

Location: Princess Anne, Md.

Enrollment: 3,600

Nickname: Hawks

Conference: Mid-Eastern Atlantic

Head Coach: Thomas C. Trotter

Collegiate Record: 28-57 (3 years)

Record at School: Same

Assistant Coaches: Paris Parham, Brian Kusnierz, Steve Golston

2002-03 Record: 5-23

2002-03 Conference Record/Finish: 5-13/9th

Starters Returning/Lost: 4/1

Lettermen Returning/Lost: 9/3

Website: www.umes.edu/athletics

2003-04 UMES Hawks Roster

Player	Ht.	Wt.	Yr.	Pos.	Hometown	ppg/rpg/apg
Jermaul Akanbi	6-2	165	So.	G	Baltimore, Md.	2.0/0.5/0.2
Greg Brown	6-0	180	So.	G	Salisbury, Md.	1.6/1.2/1.6
Jareem Dowling	6-6	235	Jr.	F	St. Croix, U.S. Virgin Islands	
Ka'Reem Horton	6-4	156	Sr.	G	Roxbury, Mass.	5.0/2.3/1.1
Antoine Joiner	6-5	180	Jr.	G	Hazel Crest, Ill.	3.9/1.8/0.6
Jason McKinnon	6-11	270	Jr.	C	Chicago, Ill.	
Tim Parham	6-9	235	So.	C	County Club Hills, Ill.	
Carl Pruitt	6-6	215	Jr.	F	Chicago, Ill.	
DeWitt Scott	6-6	200	Fr.	F	Chicago, Ill.	
Jason Scott	7-0	320	Sr.	C	Chicago, Ill.	
Lawrence Smith	5-10	150	Jr.	G	Landover, Md.	0.4/0./ 0.7
Didier Socka	6-7	225	Sr.	F	Criteil, France	4.8/4.0/0.3
Tee Trotter	5-11	180	Sr.	G	Las Cruces, N.M.	20.5/2.3/3.2
Aaron Wellington	5-11	160	So.	G	Chicago, Ill.	13.5/3.1/2.0
Kirk Wesley	6-3	190	Sr.	F	Chicago, Ill.	
Javes Wiggins	6-7	220	Sr.	F	Baltimore, Md.	5.8/5.1/0.4
Brandon Wilson	6-4	190	Fr.	G	Long Island, N.Y.	

Series History

First Meeting

Quick Facts

Location: Memphis, Tenn.

Enrollment: 20,322

Nickname: Tigers

Conference: Conference USA

Head Coach: John Calipari

Collegiate Record: 241-95 (10 years)

Record at Memphis: 71-31 (3 years)

Assistant Coaches: Tony Barbee, Ed Schilling, Derek Kellogg

2002-03 Record: 23-7

2002-03 Conference Record (Finish): 13-3/1st

Starters Returning/Lost: 3/2

Lettermen Returning/Lost: 8/4

Website: www.gotigersgo.com

2003-04 Memphis Tigers Roster

Player	Ht.	Wt.	Yr.	Pos.	Hometown	ppg/rpg/apg
Sean Banks	6-6	206	Fr.	F	Oradell, N.J.	
Arthur Barclay	6-8	256	Jr.	F	Camden, N.J.	
Antonio Burks	6-0	201	Sr.	G	Memphis, Tenn.	9.7/2.0/5.6
Rodney Carney	6-7	205	So.	F	Indianapolis, Ind.	9.8/4.8/1.1
Modibo Diarra	6-11	252	Sr.	C	Mali, West Africa	1.0/1.7/0.2
Duane Erwin	6-9	238	Jr.	F	Huntsville, Ala.	2.1/3.0/0.5
Jeremy Hunt	6-4	206	So.	G	Memphis, Tenn.	9.4/2.5/2.5
Ivan Lopez	6-8	236	Fr.	F	Aguadilla, Puerto Rico	
Simplice Njoya	6-10	225	Jr.	F	Yaounde, Cameroon	
Anthony Rice	6-4	205	Jr.	G	Atlanta, Ga.	8.8/2.8/2.4
Billy Richmond	6-5	200	Jr.	G	Memphis, Tenn.	8.5/3.5/1.8
Almamy Thiero	6-10	250	Fr.	F	Mali, West Africa	
Clyde Wade	6-0	180	So.	G	Memphis, Tenn.	1.4/0.6/1.2

Series History

Series: Illinois leads 2-1

Games at Illinois: N/A

Games at Memphis: Tied 1-1

Neutral Site: Illinois leads 1-0

Last Illinois win: 84-75 (12/29/90, at Memphis)

Last Memphis win: 77-74 (12/28/02, at Memphis)

Longest Illinois winning streak: 2 (1989-90)

Longest Illinois home winning streak: N/A

Longest Illinois road winning streak: 1 (1990)

Longest Memphis winning streak: 1 (2002) Current

Longest Memphis home winning streak: 1 (2002) Current

Longest Memphis road winning streak: N/A

Current Series Streak: Memphis W-1

Illinois Largest Winning Margin: 12 (83-71), Dec. 30, 1989, at Rosemont, Ill.

Memphis' Largest Winning Margin: 3 (77-74), Dec. 28, 2002 at Memphis, Tenn.

Weber vs. Memphis: First Meeting

Calipari vs. Illinois at Memphis: 1-0

Quick Facts

Location: Macon, Ga.
Enrollment: 7,400
Nickname: Bears
Conference: Atlantic Sun
Head Coach: Mark Slonaker
Collegiate Record: 67-104 (4 years)
Record at School: Same

Assistant Coaches: Cleveland Jackson, Jeremy Luther, Patrick Henry
2002-03 Record: 23-6
2002-03 Conference Record/Finish: 14-2/T-1st
Starters Returning/Lost: 3/3
Lettermen Returning/Lost: 11/4
Website: www.mercer.edu

2003-04 Mercer Bears Roster

Player	Ht.	Wt.	Yr.	Pos.	Hometown	ppg/rpg/apg
Ross Alacqua	5-8	160	So.	G	Alpharetta, Ga.	
Andrew Brown	6-1	180	So.	G	Pontiac, Mich.	
Wesley Duke	6-5	225	Sr.	F	Norcross, Ga.	9.3/6.7/1.3
Scott Emerson	6-9	235	Sr.	F	St. Mary's, Ga.	15.1/9.1/1.9
Will Emerson	6-10	235	So.	F	St. Mary's, Ga.	
Micalvin Hammonds	6-2	175	Fr.	G	Whigham, Ga.	
Bobby Hansen	6-9	215	Sr.	F	Belleview, Fla.	2.3/2.2/0.5
Jay January	6-2	195	Jr.	G	Wichita Falls, Texas	3.4/1.6/1.1
David Matthews	6-2	165	Jr.	G	Fayetteville, Ga.	
Tyler McCurry	5-10	180	Jr.	G	Abingdon, Ill.	1.2/0.5/1.3
James Odoms	6-5	195	Jr.	G	Gray, Ga.	
Jacob Skogen	6-4	175	Fr.	G	Lookout Mountain, Ga.	
Michael Slonaker	6-1	165	So.	G	Macon, Ga.	
Andrew Walker	6-9	245	Jr.	F	Lawrenceville, Ga.	
Delmar Wilson	6-3	190	Sr.	G/F	Miami, Fla.	

Series History

Series: Illinois leads 2-0
Games at Illinois: Illinois leads 2-0
Games at Mercer: N/A
Neutral Games: N/A
Last Illinois Win: 90-66 (12/19/94, Champaign)
Last Mercer Win: N/A
Longest Illinois win streak: 2 (1992, 94) Current
Longest Illinois home win streak: 2 (1992, 94) Current

Longest Illinois away win streak: N/A
Longest Mercer win streak: N/A
Longest Mercer home win streak: N/A
Longest Mercer away win streak: N/A
Current Series Streak: Illinois W-2
Illinois' Largest Winning Margin: 24 (90-66), Dec. 19, 1994 at Champaign
Mercer's Largest Winning Margin: N/A
Weber vs. Mercer: First Meeting
Slonaker vs. Illinois at Mercer: First Meeting

2003-04 schedule

Nov. 21   Oakland
Nov. 26   High Point
Nov. 30   at Butler
Dec. 2   North Carolina State
Dec. 6   at Vanderbilt
Dec. 13   Bowling Green
Dec. 20   Central Michigan
Dec. 22   Delaware State
Dec. 27   UCLA
Dec. 30   Boston University
Jan. 3   at Fairfield
Jan. 7   Northwestern
Jan. 11   Indiana
Jan. 17   at Michigan State
Jan. 21   at Wisconsin
Jan. 24   at Penn State
Jan. 28   Iowa
Jan. 31   at Illinois
Feb. 7   Purdue
Feb. 11   at Minnesota
Feb. 14   at Iowa
Feb. 18   Penn State
Feb. 22   Wisconsin
Feb. 24   Michigan State
Feb. 29   Ohio State
Mar. 2 or 3 at Indiana
Mar. 6 or 7 at Northwestern
Mar. 11-14 Big Ten Tournament

Quick Facts

Location: Ann Arbor, Mich.

Enrollment: 36,787

Nickname: Wolverines

Conference: Big Ten

Head Coach: Tommy Amaker

Collegiate Coaching Record: 96-86 (6 years)

Record at Michigan: 28-31 (2 years)

Assistant Coaches: Charles Ramsey, Chuck Swenson, Andy Moore

2002-03 Overall Record: 17-13

2002-03 Conference Record/Finish: 10-6/T-3rd

Starters Returning/Lost: 4/1

Letterman Returning/Lost: 10/4

Website: www.mgoblue.com

2003-04 Michigan Wolverines Roster

Player	Ht.	Wt.	Yr.	Pos.	Hometown	ppg/rpg/apg
Lester Abram	6-6	200	So.	F	Pontiac, Mich.	10.6/4.4/1.3
John Andrews	6-5	200	Fr.	F	West Bloomfield, Mich.	
Amadou Ba	6-10	250	Fr.	C	Mauritania, Africa	
Graham Brown	6-9	250	So.	F/C	Mio, Mich.	5.8/4.6/0.5
Colin Dill	6-7	240	Sr.	F	Saginaw, Mich.	
Sherrod Harrell	6-3	205	So.	G	Kalamazoo, Mich.	
Dion Harris	6-3	200	Fr.	G	Detroit, Mich.	
Daniel Horton	6-3	200	So.	G	Cedar Hill, Texas	15.2/2.3/4.5
Chris Hunter	6-11	215	So.	F/C	Gary, Ind.	
J.C. Mathis	6-8	235	Jr.	F	Brooklyn, N.Y.	
Brent Petway	6-9	200	Fr.	F	McDonough, Ga.	
Bernard Robinson Jr.	6-6	210	Sr.	F	Washington D.C.	11.7/6.1/3.4
Courtney Sims	6-10	220	Fr.	F/C	Roslindale, Mass.	
Dani Wohl	5-11	175	So.	G	West Bloomfield, Mich.	

Series History

Series: Illinois leads 75-67
Games at Illinois: Illinois leads 48-23
Games at Michigan: Michigan leads 43-27
Neutral Games: Michigan leads 1-0
Last Illinois Win: 82-79 (3/1/03, Ann Arbor)
Last Michigan Win: 95-91 2OT (1/16/00, Ann Arbor)
Longest Illinois win streak: 10 (1950-56)
Longest Illinois home win streak: 10 (1980-89)
Longest Illinois away win streak: 4 (1952-55)
Longest Michigan win streak: 9 (1992-96)

Longest Michigan home win streak: 8 (1975-82)
Longest Michigan away win streak: 4 (1992-95)
Current Series Streak: Illinois W-7
Illinois' Largest Winning Margin: 30 (96-66), Dec. 15, 1953 at Champaign
Michigan's Largest Winning Margin: 26 (42-16), Feb. 25, 1922 at Ann Arbor
Weber vs. Michigan: First Meeting
Amaker vs. Illinois all-time: 0-6

2003-04 schedule

Nov. 21	Bucknell
Nov. 25	at Kansas
Nov. 29	Indiana St.
Nov. 30	Coca-Cola Classic
Dec. 3	Duke
Dec. 6	vs. Oklahoma @ Auburn Hills
Dec. 13	vs. Kentucky @ Detroit, Mich.
Dec. 16	South Florida
Dec. 20	at UCLA
Dec. 30	Coppin State
Jan. 3	at Syracuse
Jan. 10	at Wisconsin
Jan. 14	Penn State
Jan. 17	Michigan
Jan. 21	at Northwestern
Jan. 25	at Purdue
Jan. 28	at Minnesota
Jan. 31	Indiana
Feb. 4	Iowa
Feb. 7	at Ohio State
Feb. 10	at Illinois
Feb. 14	Minnesota
Feb. 17	Purdue
Feb. 21	Northwestern
Feb. 24	at Michigan
Feb. 28	at Penn State
Mar. 2 or 3	Wisconsin
Mar. 11-14	Big Ten Tournament

Quick Facts

Location: East Lansing, Mich.

Enrollment: 44,227

Nickname: Spartans

Conference: Big Ten

Head Coach: Tom Izzo

Collegiate Coaching Record: 189-78 (8 years)

Record at Michigan State: Same

Assistant Coaches: Mark Montgomery, Dwayne Stephens, Doug Wojcik

2002-03 Overall Record: 22-13

2002-03 Conference Record/Finish: 10-6/T-3rd

Starters Returning/Lost: 3/2

Letterman Returning/Lost: 8/5

Website: www.msuspartans.com

2003-04 Michigan State Spartans Roster

Player	Ht.	Wt.	Yr.	Pos.	Hometown	ppg/rpg/apg
Maurice Ager	6-4	190	So.	G	Detroit, Mich.	6.7/2.3/0.6
Alan Anderson	6-6	220	Jr.	F	Minneapolis, Minn.	9.8/3.7/3.3
Jason Andreas	6-10	250	Sr.	C	Sugarcreek, Ohio	1.0/1.3/0.1
Tim Bograkos	6-2	195	Jr.	G	Flint, Mich.	1.6/1.5/0.8
Shannon Brown	6-3	200	Fr.	G	Maywood, Ill.	
Brandon Cotton	6-0	175	Fr.	G	Detroit, Mich.	
Paul Davis	6-11	250	So.	C	Rochester, Mich.	7.8/4.7/0.4
Anthony Hamo	6-2	210	Fr.	G	Flint, Mich.	
Andy Harvey	6-5	220	So.	F	Escanaba, Mich.	
Chris Hill	6-3	190	Jr.	G	Indianapolis, Ind.	13.7/3.4/3.7
Rashi Johnson	6-2	190	Sr.	G	Chicago, Ill.	1.0/0.8/1.0
Drew Naymick	6-10	235	Fr.	C	Muskegon, Mich.	
Delco Rowley	6-8	250	Fr.	F	Indianapolis, Ind.	
Kelvin Torbert	6-4	215	Jr.	G	Flint, Mich.	8.7/3.8/1.7
Jayson Vincent	6-4	200	So.	G	Mason, Mich.	

Series History

Series: Illinois leads 48-47

Games at Illinois: Illinois leads 31-15

Games at Michigan St.: Michigan State leads 30-16

Neutral Games: Michigan State leads 2-1

Last Illinois Win: 70-40 (2/18/03, Champaign)

Last Michigan St. Win: 68-65 (2/2/03, at East Lansing)

Longest Illinois win streak: 7 (1987-90)

Longest Illinois home win streak: 7 (1979-85)

Longest Illinois away win streak: 3 (1987-89)

Longest Michigan State win streak: 10 (1974-78)

Longest Michigan St. home win streak: 8 (1972-80)

Longest Michigan St. away win streak: 5 (1974-78)

Current Series Streak: Illinois W-1

Illinois' Largest Winning Margin: 32 (121-89), March 9, 1965 at Champaign

Michigan State's Largest Winning Margin: 25 (91-66), Jan. 30, 2000 at East Lansing

Weber vs. Michigan State: First Meeting

Izzo vs. Illinois at Michigan State: 10-6

Location: Minneapolis, Minn.

Enrollment: 45,615

Nickname: Golden Gophers

Conference: Big Ten

Head Coach: Dan Monson

Collegiate Coaching Record: 119-74 (6 years)

Record at Minnesota: 67-57 (4 years)

Assistant Coaches: Mike Petersen, Bill Walker, Vic Couch

2002-03 Overall Record: 19-14

2002-03 Conference Record (Finish): 8-8/T-6th

Starters Returning/Lost: 2/3

Letterman Returning/Lost: 6/4

Website: www.gophersports.com

2003-04 schedule

Nov 17	Missouri @ Kansas City
Nov 19	Utah or Georgia State
Nov 30	Furman
Dec 3	at Virginia
Dec 6	Western Illinois
Dec 9	Long Beach State
Dec 12	Oral Roberts
Dec 22	Duquesne
Dec 29	Nebraska
Jan 1	at Texas Tech
Jan 4	Wofford
Jan 7	at Penn State
Jan 10	Princeton
Jan 13	Iowa
Jan 17	at Ohio State
Jan 21	at Purdue
Jan 24	Indiana
Jan 28	Michigan State
Jan 31	at Northwestern
Feb 4	at Wisconsin
Feb 8	Illinois
Feb 11	Michigan
Feb 14	at Michigan State
Feb 18	at Indiana
Feb 21	Purdue
Feb 25	Ohio State
Feb 28	at Iowa
Mar 6	Penn State
Mar 11-14	Big Ten Tournament

2003-04 Minnesota Golden Gophers Roster

Player	Ht.	Wt.	Yr.	Pos.	Hometown	ppg/rpg/apg
Michael Bauer	6-8	220	Sr.	F	Hastings, Minn.	11.4/4.9/2.3
Tyree Bolden	6-5	186	Sr.	F	Milwaukee, Wis.	
Adam Boone	6-2	202	Jr.	G	Minnetonka, Minn.	
Randy Chall	6-5	215	Sr.	F	Forest Lake, Minn.	
Stan Gaines	6-7	230	So.	F	Chicago, Ill.	2.1/1.7/0.6
Jeff Hagen	6-11	265	Jr.	C	Minnetonka, Minn.	4.1/2.9/0.5
Maurice Hargrow	6-4	193	Jr.	G	St. Paul, Minn.	13.2/4.7/2.8
Wade Hokenson	5-9	170	Sr.	G	Watertown, Minn.	
Kris Humphries	6-8	240	Fr.	F	Chaska, Minn.	
Ben Johnson	6-3	185	Sr.	G	Minneapolis, Minn.	6.5/2.9/1.9
Aliou Kane	6-9	243	Fr.	C	Dallas, Texas	
Brent Lawson	6-4	200	Jr.	G	Maple Grove, Minn.	1.2/0.6/0.2
Jordan Nuness	6-4	185	Fr.	G/F	Eden Prairie, Minn.	
Aaron Robinson	5-10	165	Jr.	G	Rockford, Ill.	2.0/1.4/1.3
Matt Smriga	6-8	255	Jr.	F	Apple Valley, Minn.	
Wesley Washington	6-3	165	Fr.	G	Corona, Calif.	
Kerry Wooldridge	6-7	195	Fr.	F	San Leandro, Calif.	

Series History

Series: Illinois leads 103-60

Games at Illinois: Illinois leads 64-16

Games at Minnesota: Minnesota leads 43-37

Neutral Games: Illinois leads 2-1

Last Illinois Win: 84-60 (3/9/03, at Champaign)

Last Minnesota Win: 75-63 (2/3/99, at Minneapolis)

Longest Illinois win streak: 10 (1999-03) Current

Longest Illinois home win streak: 15 (1979-95)

Longest Illinois away win streak: 4 (four times, last 2000-2003)

Longest Minnesota win streak: 9 (1971-76)

Longest Minnesota home win streak: 6 (1970-76)

Longest Minnesota away win streak: 4 (1973-76)

Current Series Streak: Illinois W-10

Illinois' Largest Winning Margin: 36 (86-50), Feb. 11, 1968 at Champaign

Minnesota's Largest Winning Margin: 39 (42-3), Jan. 31, 1907 at Minneapolis

Weber vs. Minnesota: First Meeting

Monson vs. Illinois at Minnesota: 0-9

Quick Facts

Location: Columbia, Mo.

Enrollment: 23,666

Nickname: Tigers

Conference: Big 12

Head Coach: Quin Snyder

Collegiate Coaching Record:
84-49 (4 years)

Record at Missouri: Same

Assistant Coaches: Tony Harvey,
Lane Odom, Marcus Perez

2002-03 Overall Record: 22-11

2002-03 Conference Record/Finish:
9-7/5th

Starters Returning/Lost: 4/1

Letterman Returning/Lost: 7/4

Website: www.mutigers.com

2003-04 Missouri Tigers Roster

Player	Ht.	Wt.	Yr.	Pos.	Hometown	ppg/rpg/apg
Travon Bryant	6-9	244	Sr.	F	Long Beach, Calif.	8.9/5.8/1.1
Jason Conley	6-5	210	Jr.	G	Rockville, Md.	
Jeffrey Ferguson	6-10	245	Jr.	F/C	Toronto, Ontario	1.4/2.3/0.1
Thomas Gardner	6-5	210	Fr.	G	Portland, Ore.	
Arthur Johnson	6-9	268	Sr.	F/C	Detroit, Mich.	16.1/9.6/1.2
Linas Kleiza	6-8	245	Fr.	F/C	Rockville, Md.	
Josh Kroenke	6-4	197	Sr.	G	Columbia, Mo.	3.5/2.4/1.7
Spencer Laurie	6-1	170	Fr.	G	Springfield, Mo.	
Jimmy McKinney	6-3	200	So.	G	St. Louis, Mo.	8.6/3.8/3.4
Randy Pulley	6-2	213	Jr.	G	Raleigh, N.C.	
Rickey Paulding	6-5	218	Sr.	G/F	Detroit, Mich.	17.4/5.5/2.2
Kevin Young	6-9	275	So.	F/C	Kingston, Jamaica	2.3/3.2/0.3

Series History

Series: Illinois leads 21-12
Games at Illinois: Illinois leads 4-1
Games at Missouri: Illinois leads 3-2
Neutral Games: Illinois leads 14-9
Last Illinois Win: 85-70 (12/21/02, at St. Louis)
Last Missouri Win: 78-72 (12/21/99, at St. Louis)
Longest Illinois win streak: 8 (1983-90)
Longest Illinois home win streak: 4 (1934-77)
Longest Illinois away win streak: 2 (1932-43)
Longest Missouri win streak: 4 (1991-94)

Longest Missouri home win streak: 2 (1955-76)
Longest Missouri away win streak: 1 (1979)
Current Series Streak: Illinois W-3
Illinois' Largest Winning Margin: 28 (77-49),
    Dec. 4, 1954 at Champaign
Missouri's Largest Winning Margin: 17
    (61-44), Dec. 23, 1991, at St. Louis
Weber vs. Missouri all-time: 0-1
Snyder vs. Illinois at Missouri: 1-3

Quick Facts

Location: Chapel Hill, N.C.

Enrollment: 25,480

Nickname: Tar Heels

Conference: Atlantic Coast

Head Coach: Roy Williams

Collegiate Record: 419-101 (15 years)

Record at North Carolina: First season

Assistant Coaches: Jerod Haase, Joe Holladay, Steve Robinson

2002-03 Record: 19-16

2002-03 Conference Record (Finish): 6-10/T-6th

Starters Returning/Lost: 5/0

Lettermen Returning/Lost: 10/2

Website: www.tarheelblue.com

2003-04 North Carolina Tar Heels Roster

Player	Ht.	Wt.	Yr.	Pos.	Hometown	ppg/rpg/apg
Justin Bohlander	6-7	190	Fr.	F	Winston-Salem, N.C.	
Raymond Felton	6-1	192	So.	G	Latta, S.C.	12.9/4.1/6.7
Damion Grant	6-11	262	So.	C	Portland, Jamaica	1.6/1.5/0.0
Jackie Manuel	6-5	202	Jr.	F	West Palm Beach, Fla.	7.3/4.0/2.0
Sean May	6-8	266	So.	F/C	Bloomington, Ind.	11.4/8.1/1.0
Rashad McCants	6-4	205	So.	G/F	Asheville, N.C.	17.0/4.6/1.5
Phillip McLamb	6-6	212	Sr.	F	Charlotte, N.C.	1.0/0.3/0.2
Jonathan Miller	6-1	194	Sr.	G	Burlington, N.C.	
Wes Miller	5-11	185	So.	G	Charlotte, N.C.	
David Noel	6-6	223	So.	G/F	Durham, N.C.	5.9/3.5/1.4
Damien Price	5-11	198	Sr.	G	Greensboro, N.C.	
Byron Sanders	6-9	230	So.	F	Gulfport, Miss.	1.9/2.4/0.4
Melvin Scott	6-1	183	Jr.	G	Baltimore, Md.	6.3/1.9/1.1
Reyshawn Terry	6-8	210	Fr.	F	Winston-Salem, N.C.	
Jawad Williams	6-8	221	Jr.	F	Cleveland, Ohio	14.9/5.6/2.0

Series History

Series: Tied 2-2

Games at Illinois: Illinois leads 2-1

Games at North Carolina: UNC leads 1-0

Neutral Site: N/A

Last Illinois win: 92-65 (12/3/02, at Champaign)

Last North Carolina win: 85-74 (12/19/87, at Champaign)

Longest Illinois winning streak: 1 (2002)

Longest Illinois home winning streak: 1, (2002)

Longest Illinois road winning streak: N/A

Longest North Carolina winning streak: 2 (1986-87)

Longest North Carolina home winning streak: 1 (1986) current

Longest North Carolina road winning streak: 1 (1987)

Current Series Streak: Illinois W-1

Illinois Largest Winning Margin: 27 (92-65), Dec. 3, 2002, at Champaign

North Carolina's Largest Winning Margin: 13 (90-77) Dec. 20, 1986

Weber vs. North Carolina: First Meeting

Williams vs. Illinois at UNC: First Meeting

Northwestern

2003-04 schedule

Nov. 21 Colorado
Nov. 23 Chicago State
Nov. 25 at DePaul
Nov. 29 Northwestern State
Dec. 1   at Florida State
Dec. 3   Bucknell
Dec. 6   at Bowling Green
Dec. 17 Arizona State
Dec. 20 UIC
Sierra Providence SunClassic
Dec. 27 vs. Rutgers
Jan. 7   at Michigan
Jan. 10 at Iowa
Jan. 14 Illinois
Jan. 17 at Indiana
Jan. 21 Michigan State
Jan. 28 at Penn State
Jan. 31 Minnesota
Feb. 4   at Ohio State
Feb. 7   Wisconsin
Feb. 11 at Purdue
Feb. 14 Penn State
Feb. 21 at Michigan Stat
Feb. 25 Indiana
Feb. 28 at Illinois
March 3 Iowa
March 6 Michigan
Mar. 11-14 Big Ten Tournament

Quick Facts

Location: Evanston, Ill.
Enrollment: 7,700
Nickname: Wildcats
Conference: Big Ten
Head Coach: Bill Carmody
Collegiate Coaching Record: 131-74 (7 years)
Record at Northwestern: 39-49 (3 years)

Assistant Coaches: Paul Lee, Craig Robinson, Mitch Henderson
2002-03 Overall Record: 12-17
2002-03 Conference Record/ Finish: 3-13/10th
Starters Returning/Lost: 3/2
Letterman Returning/Lost: 7/3
Website: www.nusports.com

2003-04 Northwestern Wildcats Roster

Player	Ht.	Wt.	Yr.	Pos.	Hometown	ppg/rpg/apg
Davor Duvancic	6-8	220	Jr.	F	Split, Croatia	2.8/1.8/0.9
Mohamed Hachad	6-5	180	So.	G	Montreal, Quebec	4.3/2.1/1.5
T.J. Parker	6-2	165	So.	G	Lisle, Ill.	11.4/2.7/2.7
Evan Seacat	6-2	180	So.	G	Paoli, Ind.	3.3/0.6/0.3
Vince Scott	6-10	230	Fr.	C	Phoenix, Ariz./Greenway	
Ivan Tolic	6-9	255	So.	F/C	Split, Croatia	
Patrick Towne	6-5	220	Sr.	F	Plano, Texas	
Vedran Vukusic	6-8	230	Jr.	F	Split, Croatia	
Jitim Young	6-2	195	Sr.	G	Chicago, Ill.	13.4/5.1/2.2

Series History

Series: Illinois leads 116-33
Games at Illinois: Illinois leads 58-13
Games at Northwestern: Illinois leads 57-20
Neutral Games: Illinois leads 1-0
Last Illinois Win: 94-65 (3/14/03 at Chicago)
Last Northwestern Win: 59-46 (1/9/99 at Champaign)
Longest Illinois win streak: 16 (twice, last 1984-91)
Longest Illinois home win streak: 19 (1980-1998)
Longest Illinois away win streak: 9 (1946-55)
Longest Northwestern win streak: 3 (twice, last 1966-67)

Longest Northwestern home win streak: 3 (1966-68)
Longest Northwestern away win streak: 2 (three times, last 1959-61)
Current Series Streak: Illinois W-8
Illinois' Largest Winning Margin: 42 (twice)
 Feb. 27, 1943, at Chicago, 86-44;
 March 8, 1995, at Champaign, 99-57
Northwestern's Largest Winning Margin: 16 (88-72), March 8, 1958, at Evanston)
Weber vs. Northwestern: 0-0
Carmody vs. Illinois at Northwestern: 0-5

Quick Facts

Location: Columbus, Ohio

Enrollment: 55,043

Nickname: Buckeyes

Conference: Big Ten

Head Coach: Jim O'Brien

Collegiate Coaching Record: 354-289 (21 years)

Record at Ohio State: 119-72 (6 years)

Assistant Coaches: Rick Boyages, Monte Mathis, LaMonta Stone

2002-03 Overall Record: 17-15

2002-03 Conference Record (Finish): 7-9/T-8th

Starters Returning/Lost: 3/2

Letterman Returning/Lost: 11/7

Website: www.ohiostatebuckeyes.com

2003-04 schedule

Nov. 21	San Francisco
Nov. 24	San Diego St.
Nov. 26	TBA Maui, HI
Dec. 3	Georgia Tech
Dec. 6	Virginia Tech
Dec. 13	Samford
Dec. 17	Furman
Dec. 20	at Seton Hall
Dec. 23	Eastern Illinois
Dec. 28	Dartmouth
Dec. 30	Maryland-Baltimore County
Jan. 4	Texas Tech
Jan. 7	at Illinois
Jan. 10	at Penn St.
Jan. 17	Minnesota
Jan. 20	Indiana
Jan. 24	at Iowa
Jan. 28	Wisconsin
Jan. 31	at Purdue
Feb. 4	Northwestern
Feb. 7	Michigan St.
Feb. 14	at Wisconsin
Feb. 18	Iowa
Feb. 21	at Indiana
Feb. 25	at Minnesota
Feb. 29	at Michigan
Mar. 3	Penn St.
Mar. 6 or 7	Illinois
Mar. 11-14	Big Ten Tournament

2003-04 Ohio State Buckeyes Roster

Player	Ht.	Wt.	Yr.	Pos.	Hometown	ppg/rpg/apg
Charles Bass	6-9	190	So.	C/F	University Park, Ill.	0.6/1.2/0.1
Rick Billings	6-3	210	So.	G	Detroit, Mich.	
Brandon Fuss-Cheatham	6-1	200	Jr.	G	Beaver Falls, Pa.	1.6/2.4/1.5
Nick Dials	6-1	175	Fr.	G	New Haven, Ohio	
Terence Dials	6-9	260	So.	F/C	Youngstown, Ohio	
Ivan Harris	6-8	220	Fr.	F	Springfield, Ohio	
Shun Jenkins	6-6	240	Sr.	F	Albany, Ga.	5.1/6.1/0.3
Matt Marinchick	6-10	260	Jr.	C	Hudson, Ohio	1.3/0.6/0.2
Velimir Radinovic	7-0	250	Sr.	C	Toronto, Ontario	9.3/6.1/0.5
Shaun Smith	5-10	180	Sr.	G	Cincinnati, Ohio	
Tony Stockman	6-1	180	Jr.	G	Medina, Ohio	
J.J. Sullinger	6-5	200	So.	G	Columbus, Ohio	
Matt Sylvester	6-7	205	So.	F	Loveland, Ohio	5.7/2.8/1.4

Series History

Series: Illinois leads 97-59

Games at Illinois: Illinois leads 57-21

Games at Ohio State: Illinois leads 38-37

Neutral Games: Illinois leads 2-1

Last Illinois Win: 72-59 (3/16/03, at Chicago)

Last Ohio State Win: 94-88 (3/9/02, at Indianapolis)

Longest Illinois win streak: 12 (1950-56)

Longest Illinois home win streak: 13 (1945-59)

Longest Illinois away win streak: 6 (1993-98)

Longest Ohio State win streak: 7 (1977-80)

Longest Ohio State home win streak: 6 (1967-73)

Longest Ohio State away win streak: 4 (1977-80)

Current Series Streak: Illinois W-2

Illinois' Largest Winning Margin: 47 (111-64), Feb. 11, 1956, at Champaign

Ohio State's Largest Winning Margin: 34 (89-55), Jan. 19, 1991, at Columbus

Weber vs. Ohio State: First Meeting

O'Brien vs. Illinois at Ohio State: 5-6

Penn State

Wednesday, Jan. 21 at Champaign, 8 p.m.
ESPN+ Local
Saturday, Feb. 21 at State College, 3 p.m.
ESPN

2003-04 schedule

Nov. 23   Georgetown
Nov. 26   St. Francis
Nov. 29   at Buffalo
Dec. 3   Cleveland State
Dec. 6   at Pittsburgh
Dec. 10   Rutgers
Dec. 13   at Temple
Dec. 20   St. Francis (NY)
Dec. 28   vs. Arkansas State
Dec. 29   TBA
Jan. 3   Bucknell
Jan. 7   Minnesota
Jan. 10   Ohio State
Jan. 14   at Michigan State
Jan. 21   at Illinois
Jan. 24   Michigan
Jan. 28   Northwestern
Jan. 31   at Iowa
Feb. 4   Purdue
Feb. 11   Indiana
Feb. 14   at Northwestern
Feb. 18   at Michigan
Feb. 21   Illinois
Feb. 25   at Wisconsin
Feb. 28   Michigan State
Mar. 3   at Ohio State
Mar. 6   at Minnesota
Mar. 11-14   Big Ten Tournament

Quick Facts

Location: University Park, Pa.
Enrollment: 41,050
Nickname: Nittany Lions
Conference: Big Ten
Head Coach: Ed DeChellis
Collegiate Coaching Record: 105-93 (7 years)
Record at Penn State: First season

Assistant Coaches: James Johnson, Kurt Kanaskie, Hilliary Scott
2002-03 Overall Record: 7-21
2002-03 Conference Record/Finish: 2-14/11th
Starters Returning/Lost: 3/2
Letterman Returning/Lost: 9/3
Website: www.GoPSUsports.com

2003-04 Penn State Nittany Lions Roster

Player	Ht.	Wt.	Yr.	Pos.	Hometown	ppg/rpg/apg
Brandon Cameron	6-0	171	So.	G	Gary, Ind.	1.7/1.1/1.3
Ndu Egekeze	6-6	230	Sr.	F	Augusta, Ga.	2.5/1.5/0.1
Kevin Fellows	6-10	244	Jr.	C	Meridian, Idaho	1.0/0.6/0.2
Rob Fletcher	6-5	210	Sr.	G/F	Pittsburgh, Penn.	
Jan Jagla	7-0	232	Jr.	F	Berlin, Germany	9.3/6.8/0.9
Aaron Johnson	6-9	240	So.	F	Exton, Penn.	8.3/7.5/0.5
John Kelly	6-11	250	Fr.	C	West Milford, N.J.	
Ben Luber	6-0	160	Fr.	G	Richboro, Penn.	
Jason McDougald	6-9	205	Jr.	F	Lewisville, N.C.	2.2/1.0/0.2
Deforrest Riley	6-6	200	So.	G/F	Cincinatti, Ohio	7.9/2.4/2.0
Marlon Smith	6-0	186	Fr.	G	Bronx, N.Y.	
Robert Summers	6-11	232	So.	C	Gahanna, Ohio	3.9/4.0/0.4

Series History

Series: Illinois leads 14-6
Games at Illinois: Illinois leads 7-2
Games at Penn State: Illinois leads 6-3
Neutral Games: Tied 1-1
Last Illinois Win: 75-63 (1/25/03, at State College)
Last Penn St. Win: 98-95 (1/31/01, at State College)
Longest Illinois win streak: 5 (1993-95)
Longest Illinois home win streak: 4 (1993-97)
Longest Illinois away win streak: 3 (1997-2000)
Longest Penn St. win streak: 3 (1942-91)

Longest Penn St. home win streak: 1 (three times, last 2001)
Longest Penn St. away win streak: 1 (twice, last 1999)
Current Series Streak: Illinois W-2
Illinois' Largest Winning Margin: 32 (92-60), Jan. 20, 2001, at Champaign
Penn State's Largest Winning Margin: 10 (78-68), Dec. 5, 1990, at University Park
Weber vs. Penn State: First Meeting
DeChellis vs. Illinois: First Meeting

Quick Facts

Location: Providence, R.I.
Enrollment: 3,700
Nickname: Friars
Conference: Big East
Head Coach: Tim Welsh
Collegiate Coaching Record:
151-98 (8 years)
Record at Providence: 81-73
(5 years)

Assistant Coaches: Steve DeMeo, Phil Seymore, Bob Walsh
Basketball Office Telephone: (401) 865-2266
2002-03 Overall Record: 18-14
2002-03 Conference Record/Finish: 8-8/3rd East Division
Starters Returning/Lost: 5/0
Letterman Returning/Lost: 10/4
Website: www.friars.com

2003-04 Providence Friars Roster

Player	Ht.	Wt.	Yr.	Pos.	Hometown	ppg/rpg/apg
Chris Anrin	6-7	220	Sr.	F	Varmdo, Sweden	2.9/0.7/0.1
Dwight Brewington	6-5	195	Fr.	G	Lynn, Mass.	
Gerald Brown	6-4	190	Fr.	G	Baltimore, Md.	
Marcus Douthit	6-10	235	Sr.	C	Syracuse, N.Y.	5.1/4.6/1.5
Ryan Gomes	6-7	245	Jr.	F/C	Waterbury, Conn.	18.4/9.7/2.1
Herbert Hill	6-9	220	Fr.	F	Kinston, N.C.	
Sheiku Kabba	6-3	200	Sr.	G	Bronx, N.Y.	18.1/8.5/2.4
Tuukka Kotti	6-9	220	Jr.	F	Forssa, Finland	7.7/3.6/1.6
Maris Laksa	6-9	230	Sr.	F	Ventspils, Latvia	8.5/2.4/1.2
Donnie McGrath	6-4	190	So.	G	Katonah, N.Y.	9.1/2.1/4.3
Abdul Mills	6-4	195	Sr.	G	Brooklyn, N.Y.	
Jeff Parmer	6-7	230	Fr.	F	Niagara Falls, N.Y.	
Rob Sanders	6-6	215	Jr.	F	New London, Conn.	7.4/3.8/0.7

Series History

Series: Providence leads 1-0
Games at Illinois: N/A
Games at Providence: N/A
Neutral Games: Providence leads 1-0
Last Illinois Win: N/A
Last Providence Win: 81-79 (12/28/65, at New York City)
Longest Illinois win streak: N/A
Longest Illinois home win streak: N/A
Longest Illinois away win streak: N/A

Longest Providence win streak: 1 (1965) current
Longest Providence home win streak: N/A
Longest Providence away win streak: N/A
Current Series Streak: Providence W-1
Illinois' Largest Winning Margin: N/A
Providence Largest Winning Margin: 2 (81-79), Dec. 28, 1965, at New York City
Weber vs. Providence: First Meeting
Welsh vs. Illinois at Providence: First Meeting

Purdue

Saturday, Jan. 10, 2004 at Champaign, Ill., 3:30 p.m.
ESPN+ Regional
Saturday or Sunday, March 2 or 3, 2004 at West Lafayette, Ind., TBA

2003-04 schedule

Nov. 23	Samford
Nov. 27	vs. Texas State @ Anchorage, Alaska
Nov. 28-29	TBA
Dec. 3	Clemson
Dec. 6	Chicago State
Dec. 11	at Oklahoma
Dec. 13	vs. Central Mich @ Indianapolis
Dec. 20	IPFW
Dec. 21	Miami (Ohio) or SMU
Dec. 27	Evansville
Dec. 30	at Colorado St
Jan. 3	at Baylor
Jan. 7	at Iowa
Jan. 10	at Illinois
Jan. 14	Wisconsin
Jan. 21	Minnesota
Jan. 25	Michigan St
Jan. 27	at Indiana
Jan. 31	Ohio St
Feb. 4	at Penn St
Feb. 7	at Michigan
Feb. 11	Northwestern
Feb. 14	Indiana
Feb. 17	at Michigan St
Feb. 21	at Minnesota
Feb. 29	at Wisconsin
Mar. 2	Illinois
Mar. 6	Iowa
Mar. 11-14	Big Ten Tournament

Quick Facts

Location: West Lafayette, Ind.
Enrollment: 37,871
Nickname: Boilermakers
Conference: Big Ten
Head Coach: Gene Keady
Collegiate Coaching Record: 526-254 (25 years)
Record at Purdue: 488-224 (23 years)

Assistant Coaches: Tracy Webster, Todd Foster, Cuonzo Martin
2002-03 Overall Record: 19-11
2002-03 Conference Record/ Finish: 10-6/T-3rd
Starters Returning/Lost: 4/1
Letterman Returning/Lost: 12/2
Website: www.purduesports.com

2003-04 Purdue Boilermakers Roster

Player	Ht.	Wt.	Yr.	Pos.	Hometown	ppg/rpg/apg
Chris Booker	6-10	247	Sr.	F	Fort Worth, Texas	9.4/5.7/0.9
Melvin Buckley	6-7	200	So.	G/F	Chicago, Ill.	4.1/1.9/0.2
Brett Buscher	6-8	247	Sr.	F	Chesterton, Ind.	5.9/2.9/0.3
Matt Carroll	6-8	233	So.	F	Aurora, Colo.	
Andrew Ford	6-2	197	Jr.	G	West Lafayette, Ind.	0.8/0.5/0.1
Kevin Garrity	6-11	250	Sr.	C	North Brunswick, N.J.	0.8/0.5/0.1
Chris Hartley	6-4	185	Fr.	G	Noblesville, Ind.	
Ivan Kartelo	6-11	265	Sr.	C	Split, Croatia	3.0/2.7/0.6
Matt Kiefer	6-10	225	So.	F	Evansville, Ind.	3.5/3.0/0.9
Adam Liddell	6-7	205	Fr.	G/F	DeKalb, Ind.	
Kenneth Lowe	6-3	197	Sr.	G	Gary, Ind.	11.6/2.4/2.0
Brandon McKnight	6-2	183	Jr.	G	South Bend, Ind.	5.4/2.3/2.5
Ije Nwankwo	6-7	260	Fr.	F	Ann Arbor, Mich.	
Austin Parkinson	6-0	197	Sr.	G	Kokomo, Ind.	0.9/1.1/1.9
David Teague	6-5	183	So.	G	Indianapolis, Ind.	5.7/2.2/0.4

Series History

Series: Purdue leads 84-77
Games at Illinois: Illinois leads 51-29
Games at Purdue: Purdue leads 54-25
Neutral Games: Tied at 1-1
Last Illinois Win: 75-62 (1/22/03, at Champaign)
Last Purdue Win: 70-61 (2/15/03, at West Lafayette)
Longest Illinois win streak: 11 (1950-56)
Longest Illinois home win streak: 13 (1941-61)
Longest Illinois away win streak: 5 (1951-56)
Longest Purdue win streak: 13 (1967-75)

Longest Purdue home win streak: 14 (1964-80)
Longest Purdue away win streak: 6 (twice; last 1995-2000)
Current Series Streak: Purdue W-1
Illinois' Largest Winning Margin: 44 (98-54), Feb. 21, 1948, at Champaign
Purdue's Largest Winning Margin: 34 (83-49), Feb. 14, 1970, at West Lafayette
Weber vs. Purdue: First Meeting
Keady vs. Illinois at Purdue: 24-20

TEMPLE UNIVERSITY

Quick Facts

Location: Philadelphia, Pa.

Enrollment: 30,000

Nickname: Owls

Conference: Atlantic 10

Head Coach: John Chaney

Collegiate Coaching Record: 693-269 (31 years)

Record at Temple: 468-210 (21 years)

Assistant Coaches: Bill Ellerbee, Dan Leibovitz, Mark Macon

2002-03 Overall Record: 18-16

2002-03 Conference Record/Finish: 10-6/2nd

Starters Returning/Lost: 2/3

Letterman Returning/Lost: 4/4

Website: www.owlsports.com

2003-04 Temple Owls Roster

Player	Ht.	Wt.	Yr.	Pos.	Hometown	ppg/rpg/apg
Wilbur Allen	6-4	200	So.	G	Irmo, S.C.	0.3/0.2/0.2
Micheal Blackshear	6-6	215	So.	F	Philadelphia, Pa.	
Keith Butler	7-0	250	So.	C	West Medford, Mass.	
Tyreek Byard	6-5	175	Fr.	G	Philadelphia, Pa.	
Maurice Collins	6-5	205	Fr.	G	Philadelphia, Pa.	
Dion Dacons	6-6	210	Fr.	F	Statesville, N.C.	
David Hawkins	6-4	215	Jr.	G	Washington, D.C.	16.9/4.3/2.8
Nehemiah Ingram	6-8	250	Jr.	F	Milledgeville, Ga.	
Antywane Robinson	6-8	210	Fr.	F	Charlotte, N.C.	
Dustin Salisbery	6-5	205	Fr.	G	Lancaster, Pa.	
Mario Taybron	6-3	185	Fr.	G	Hampton, Va.	

Series History

Series: Illinois leads 4-2
Games at Illinois: Illinois leads 1-0
Games at Temple: Temple leads 2-1
Neutral Games: Illinois leads 2-0
Last Illinois Win: 70-54 (12/14/02, Chicago)
Last Temple Win: 92-56 (12/10/91, Philadelphia)
Longest Illinois win streak: 3 (1940-1989)
Longest Illinois home win streak: 1 (2002) Current
Longest Illinois away win streak: 1 (1940)

Longest Temple win streak: 1 (1991)
Longest Temple home win streak: 1 (1991)
Longest Temple away win streak: N/A
Current Series Streak: Illinois W-1
Illinois' Largest Winning Margin: 17 (78-61), Dec. 16, 1989, at Champaign
Temple Largest Winning Margin: 36 (92-56), Dec. 10, 1991, at Philadelphia
Weber vs. Temple: First Meeting
Chaney vs. Illinois at Temple: 1-3

Western Illinois

Quick Facts

Location: Macomb, Ill.

Enrollment: 13,450

Nickname: Leathernecks

Conference: Mid-Continent

Head Coach: Derek Thomas

Collegiate Record: First season

Record at Western Illinois: First season

Assistant Coaches: David James, Jeff Guin, Charles Manno

2002-03 Record: 12-16

2002-03 Conference Record (Finish): 3-11 (10th)

Starters Returning/Lost: 1/5

Lettermen Returning/Lost: 6/7

Website: www.wiuathletics.com

2003-04 WIU Leathernecks Roster

Player	Ht.	Wt.	Yr.	Pos.	Hometown	ppg/rpg/apg
Keith Archie	6-7	240	Jr.	F	Dolton, Ill.	
Bobby Carter	6-3	185	Sr.	G	Oklahoma City, Okla.	3.3/1.3/1.0
Andre Charles	6-8	220	Sr.	F/C	Chicago, Ill.	3.3/2.2/0.2
Doyle Cole	6-5	185	Jr.	G	Los Angeles, Calif.	
David Genslinger	6-9	215	Fr.	F/C	Palos Park, Ill.	
T.J. Gray	5-9	160	Fr.	G	Chicago, Ill.	
Ray Harris	6-2	185	Sr.	G	Sacramento, Calif.	7.4/2.4/3.0
Michael Haywood	6-1	190	Jr.	G	Carbondale, Ill.	
Anthony Lenior	6-6	225	Jr.	F	Evanston, Ill.	
Will Lewis	6-6	215	Jr.	F	Chicago, Ill.	11.4/5.4/1.4
Brian Schmidt	6-0	170	Fr.	G	St. Charles, Ill.	
Jawaan Stalling	6-0	170	Fr.	G	Chicago, Ill.	
J.D. Summers	6-3	200	Sr.	G	Quincy, Ill.	12.6/4.7/2.5
Barry Welsh	6-0	165	Jr.	G	Abingdon, Ill.	3.9/1.7/3.1

Series History

Series: Illinois leads 4-0

Games at Illinois: Illinois leads 4-0

Games at Western Illinois: N/A

Neutral Site: N/A

Last Illinois win: 85-56 (12/01/02, at Champaign)

Last Western Illinois win: N/A

Longest Illinois winning streak: 4 current

Longest Illinois home winning streak: 4 current

Longest Illinois road winning streak: N/A

Longest Western Illinois winning streak: N/A

Longest Western Illinois home winning streak: N/A

Longest Western Illinois road winning streak: N/A

Current Series Streak: Illlinois W-4

Illinois Largest Winning Margin: 36 (98-62), Dec. 16, 2001, at Champaign, Ill.

Western Illinois' Largest Winning Margin: N/A

Weber vs. Western Illinois: First Meeting

Thomas vs. Illinois: First Meeting

Wisconsin

2003-04 schedule

Nov. 21 at Pennsylvania
Nov. 25 Eastern Illinois
Nov. 29 Rutgers
Dec. 2   at Maryland
Dec. 6   Detroit
Dec. 10 UW-Green Bay
Dec. 13 UW-Milwaukee
Dec. 20 Marquette
Dec. 27 vs. Ohio
Dec. 30 at Alabama
Jan. 3   College of Charleston
Jan. 6   Indiana
Jan. 10 Michigan State
Jan. 14 at Purdue
Jan. 21 Michigan
Jan. 24 Illinois
Jan. 28 at Ohio State
Feb. 4   Minnesota
Feb. 7   at Northwestern
Feb. 11 at Iowa
Feb. 14 Ohio State
Feb. 18 at Illinois
Feb. 22 at Michigan
Feb. 25 Penn State
Feb. 29 Purdue
Mar. 2 or 3 at Michigan State
Mar. 6 or 7 at Indiana
Mar. 11-14 Big Ten Tournament

Quick Facts

Location: Madison, Wis.

Enrollment: 41,522

Nickname: Badgers

Conference: Big Ten

Head Coach: Bo Ryan

Collegiate Coaching Record:
426-124 (18 years)

Record at Wisconsin: 43-21
(2 years)

Assistant Coaches: Rob Jeter, Gary Close, Greg Gard

2002-03 Overall Record: 24-8

2002-03 Conference Record/
Finish: 12-4/1st

Starters Returning/Lost: 4/1

Letterman Returning/Lost: 9/1

Website: www.uwbadgers.com

2003-04 Wisconsin Badgers Roster

Player	Ht.	Wt.	Yr.	Pos.	Hometown	ppg/rpg/apg
Brian Butch	6-11	220	Fr.	F/C	Appleton, Wis.	
Sharif Chambliss	6-1	175	Sr.	G	Racine, Wis.	
Jason Chappell	6-10	230	So.	F/C	New Berlin, Wis.	
Clayton Hanson	6-5	185	Jr.	G	Reedsburg, Wis.	2.1/0.5/0.1
Devin Harris	6-3	175	Jr.	G	Milwaukee, Wis.	12.7/4.6/3.1
Andreas Helmigk	6-9	245	So.	F	Klagenfurt, Austria	1.8/1.2/0.5
Ray Nixon	6-8	220	So.	F	Whitefish Bay, Wis.	
Dave Mader	7-0	260	Sr.	C	Appleton, Wis.	2.5/2.1/0.4
Zach Morley	6-8	220	Jr.	F	Maryville, Mo.	
Freddie Owens	6-2	185	Sr.	G	Milwaukee, Wis.	10.3/1.8/1.7
Kammron Taylor	6-2	165	Fr.	G	Minneapolis, Minn.	
Alando Tucker	6-5	195	So.	G/F	Lockport, Ill.	12.0/5.9/1.1
Ike Ukawuba	6-3	175	Sr.	G	Chicago, Ill.	
Boo Wade	6-3	185	So.	G	Milwaukee, Wis.	3.3/1.8/1.8
Mike Wilkinson	6-8	240	Jr.	F	Blue Mounds, Wis.	10.3/6.8/1.6

Series History

Series: Illinois leads 101-66
Games at Illinois: Illinois leads 64-17
Games at Wisconsin: Wisconsin leads 49-36
Neutral Games: Illinois leads 1-0
Last Illinois Win: 69-63 (1/11/03, at Champaign)
Last Wisconsin Win: 60-59 (3/5/03, at Madison)
Longest Illinois win streak: 16 (1981-1989)
Longest Illinois home win streak: 13 (1982-1994)
Longest Illinois away win streak: 10 (1979-1988)
Longest Wisconsin win streak: 6 (1912-1914)

Longest Wisconsin home win streak: 9 (1906-1914)
Longest Wisconsin away win streak: 3
    (twice, last 1928-1931)
Current Series Streak: Wisconsin W-1
Illinois' Largest Winning Margin: 39 (93-54),
    February 16, 1959 at Champaign
Wisconsin's Largest Winning Margin: 34 (47-13),
    February 1, 1907 at Madison
Weber vs. Wisconsin: First Meeting
Ryan vs. Illinois at Wisconsin: 2-2

Victor Chukwudebe was a four-year letterman for Lon Kruger's Illini teams from 1997-2000. The All-Stater from Springfield served as team captain his junior and senior seasons. Number 00 was a solid defender and rebounder and could score inside or out.

What are you doing these days?

I'm working security at my old high school [Lanphier] back here in Springfield. I monitor in-house suspensions and that kind of stuff. I'm dealing with students all day. I'm also going to work as an assistant on the basketball team. My coach [Craig Patton] retired after last season to spend more time with his family, so James Youngman is the new coach. He's from Peoria and was coach at Abingdon and Highland.

What's your greatest memory of your time spent at UI?

Oh, that's easy: getting my degree. I graduated in 2000 with a degree in sports management. I'd like to work in the sports world, preferably in the front office somewhere. Senior night for basketball was also a great time. It was the first time the whole family was able to be there together.

Which of your former teammates do you stay in touch with?

Joe Cross. Nate Mast. I ran into Jerry Gee over the summer. Arias Davis. I talked to Sergio [McClain]. Arch [Robert Archibald]. Nate's working as an architect in West Palm Beach. He's getting married next year. So is Arch.

Do you still play basketball?

Not much. I played overseas a couple of years after I graduated. I played in Rio, Brazil, and in Saskatchewan. It was different.

Who's your favorite current Illini?

I like them all. I get updates on them when I can and watch them on TV when I can. I also keep up on Brian Cook 'cause he's from close to home. I'm happy for him.

Have you met Coach Weber?

I met him once last year in Springfield. He seems like a great person and coach. He's always done a good job at Southern so I'm anxious to see what he can do this season.

NOVEMBER

17 Missouri-Kansas City at MINNESOTA [16]
19 MINNESOTA vs. Utah/Georgia State [16]
21 UNC-Greensboro at INDIANA
   Oakland at MICHIGAN
   Bucknell at MICHIGAN STATE
   OHIO STATE at San Francisco
   WISCONSIN at Penn
22 Western Illinois at ILLINOIS
23 UNC-Asheville at IOWA
   Chicago State at NORTHWESTERN
   Georgetown at PENN STATE
   Samford at PURDUE
24 INDIANA at Vanderbilt
   OHIO STATE vs. TBD [18]
25 Drake at IOWA
   MICHIGAN STATE at Kansas
   NORTHWESTERN at DePaul
   OHIO STATE vs. TBD [18]
   Eastern Illinois at WISCONSIN
26 Mercer at ILLINOIS
   MINNESOTA vs. TBD [16] [12]
   OHIO STATE vs. TBD [18]
   St. Francis (Pa.) at PENN STATE
27 PURDUE vs. Texas State [21]
28 MINNESOTA vs. TBD [16] [12]
   PURDUE vs. TBD [21]
29 ILLINOIS at Temple
   INDIANA vs. Xavier [7]
   IOWA vs. Louisville [7]
   Penn at MICHIGAN STATE [13]
   NW State (La.) at NORTHWESTERN
   PENN STATE at Buffalo
   PURDUE vs. TBD [21]
   Rutgers at WISCONSIN
30 MICHIGAN vs. Butler [11]
   DePaul/Ind. St. at MICHIGAN ST. [13]
   Furman at MINNESOTA

DECEMBER

1 NORTHWESTERN at Florida State [1]
2 ILLINOIS vs. North Carolina [1] [2]
   INDIANA at Wake Forest [1]
   Wisconsin-Green Bay at IOWA

North Carolina State at MICHIGAN [1]
WISCONSIN at Maryland [1]
3 Duke at MICHIGAN STATE [1]
   MINNESOTA at Virginia [1]
   Bucknell at NORTHWESTERN
   Georgia Tech at OHIO STATE [1]
   Cleveland State at PENN STATE
   Clemson at PURDUE [1]
5 Eastern Washington at IOWA [9]
6 ILLINOIS vs. Arkansas [4]
   Missouri at INDIANA
   N. Illinois/Illinois-Chicago at IOWA [9]
   MICHIGAN at Vanderbilt
   MICHIGAN STATE vs. Oklahoma [14]
   Western Illinois at MINNESOTA
   NORTHWESTERN at Bowling Green
   OHIO STATE vs. Virginia Tech [19]
   PENN STATE at Pittsburgh
   Chicago State at PURDUE
   Detroit at WISCONSIN
9 ILLINOIS vs. Providence [3]
   IOWA at Northern Iowa
   Long Beach State at MINNESOTA
10 INDIANA at Notre Dame
   Rutgers at PENN STATE
   UW-Green Bay at WISCONSIN
11 Maryland-Eastern Shore at ILLINOIS
   PURDUE at Oklahoma
12 Oral Roberts at MINNESOTA
13 Memphis at ILLINOIS
   Butler at INDIANA
   Bowling Green at MICHIGAN
   MICHIGAN STATE vs. Kentucky [15]
   Samford at OHIO STATE
   PENN STATE at Temple
   PURDUE vs. Central Michigan [22]
   UW-Milwaukee at WISCONSIN
16 South Florida at MICHIGAN STATE
17 Arizona State at NORTHWESTERN
   Furman at OHIO STATE
20 INDIANA vs. Kentucky [8]
   Central Michigan at MICHIGAN
   MICHIGAN STATE at UCLA
   NORTHWESTERN at Illinois-Chicago
   OHIO STATE at Seton Hall

St. Francis (N.Y.) at PENN STATE
IPFW at PURDUE [23]
Marquette at WISCONSIN
21 SMU/Miami (Ohio) at PURDUE [23]
22 IOWA vs. Texas Tech [10]
   Delaware State at MICHIGAN
   Duquesne at MINNESOTA
23 ILLINOIS vs. Missouri [5]
   Morehead State at INDIANA
   Eastern Illinois at OHIO STATE
27 UCLA at MICHIGAN
   NORTHWESTERN vs. Rutgers [17]
   Evansville at PURDUE
   WISCONSIN vs. Ohio [24]
28 N'WESTERN vs. UTEP/Miss. Valley St. [17]
   Dartmouth at OHIO STATE
   PENN STATE vs. Arkansas State [20]
29 INDIANA at North Texas
   Nebraska at MINNESOTA
   PENN STATE vs. TBD [20]
30 ILLINOIS vs. Illinois-Chicago [6]
   Eastern Illinois at IOWA
   Boston University at MICHIGAN
   Coppin State at MICHIGAN STATE
   MD-Baltimore County at OHIO STATE
   PURDUE at Colorado State
   WISCONSIN at Alabama

JANUARY

1 MINNESOTA at Texas Tech
3 Illinois State at ILLINOIS
   Temple at INDIANA
   IOWA at Missouri
   MICHIGAN vs. Fairfield [12]
   MICHIGAN STATE at Syracuse
   Bucknell at PENN STATE
   PURDUE at Baylor
   College of Charleston at WISCONSIN
4 Wofford at MINNESOTA
   Texas Tech at OHIO STATE
6 INDIANA at WISCONSIN
7 OHIO STATE at ILLINOIS
   PURDUE at IOWA
   MINNESOTA at PENN STATE
   NORTHWESTERN at MICHIGAN

10	MICHIGAN STATE at WISCONSIN
	OHIO STATE at PENN STATE
	NORTHWESTERN at IOWA
	PURDUE at ILLINOIS
	Princeton at MINNESOTA
11	INDIANA at MICHIGAN
13	IOWA at MINNESOTA
14	WISCONSIN at PURDUE
	PENN STATE at MICHIGAN STATE
	ILLINOIS at NORTHWESTERN
17	IOWA at ILLINOIS
	MICHIGAN at MICHIGAN STATE
	NORTHWESTERN at INDIANA
	MINNESOTA at OHIO STATE
20	INDIANA at OHIO STATE
21	MICHIGAN at WISCONSIN
	MICHIGAN ST. at NORTHWESTERN
	PENN STATE at ILLINOIS
	MINNESOTA at PURDUE
	IOWA at Iowa State
24	ILLINOIS at WISCONSIN
	INDIANA at MINNESOTA
	MICHIGAN at PENN STATE
	OHIO STATE at IOWA
25	MICHIGAN STATE at PURDUE
27	PURDUE at INDIANA
28	IOWA at MICHIGAN
	MICHIGAN STATE at MINNESOTA
	NORTHWESTERN at PENN STATE
	WISCONSIN at OHIO STATE
31	MICHIGAN at ILLINOIS
	INDIANA at MICHIGAN STATE

	PENN STATE at IOWA
	MINNESOTA at NORTHWESTERN
	OHIO STATE at PURDUE

FEBRUARY

3	ILLINOIS at INDIANA
4	IOWA at MICHIGAN STATE
	MINNESOTA at WISCONSIN
	NORTHWESTERN at OHIO STATE
	PURDUE at PENN STATE
7	MICHIGAN STATE at OHIO STATE
	IOWA at INDIANA
	PURDUE at MICHIGAN
	WISCONSIN at NORTHWESTERN
8	ILLINOIS at MINNESOTA
10	MICHIGAN STATE at ILLINOIS
11	INDIANA at PENN STATE
	WISCONSIN at IOWA
	MICHIGAN at MINNESOTA
	NORTHWESTERN at PURDUE
14	PENN STATE at NORTHWESTERN
	OHIO STATE at WISCONSIN
	INDIANA at PURDUE
	MICHIGAN at IOWA
	MINNESOTA at MICHIGAN STATE
17	PURDUE at MICHIGAN STATE
18	WISCONSIN at ILLINOIS
	PENN STATE at MICHIGAN
	MINNESOTA at INDIANA
	IOWA at OHIO STATE
21	ILLINOIS at PENN STATE

	NORTHWESTERN at MICHIGAN ST.
	OHIO STATE at INDIANA
	PURDUE at MINNESOTA
22	WISCONSIN at MICHIGAN
24	MICHIGAN STATE at MICHIGAN
25	ILLINOIS at IOWA
	INDIANA at NORTHWESTERN
	OHIO STATE at MINNESOTA
	PENN STATE at WISCONSIN
28	MICHIGAN STATE at PENN STATE
	NORTHWESTERN at ILLINOIS
	MINNESOTA at IOWA
29	OHIO STATE at MICHIGAN
	PURDUE at WISCONSIN

MARCH

2/3	ILLINOIS at PURDUE
2/3	MICHIGAN at INDIANA
2/3	WISCONSIN at MICHIGAN STATE
3	PENN STATE at OHIO STATE
	IOWA at NORTHWESTERN
6	IOWA at PURDUE
	PENN STATE at MINNESOTA
6/7	MICHIGAN at NORTHWESTERN
6/7	ILLINOIS at OHIO STATE
6/7	WISCONSIN at INDIANA

Times local to site—All times and dates are subject to change

Last updated on Sept. 24, 2003

SCHEDULE KEY

[1] - Big Ten/ACC Challenge

[2] - at Greensboro, N.C.

[3] - Jimmy V. Classic at Madison Square Garden in New York, N.Y.

[4] - at United Center in Chicago, Ill.

[5] - Busch Braggin' Rights at Savvis Center in St. Louis, Mo.

[6] - at United Center in Chicago, Ill.

[7] - Wooden Tradition at Conseco Fieldhouse in Indianapolis, Ind.

[8] - at RCA Dome in Indianapolis, Ind.

[9] - Gazette Hawkeye Challenge in Iowa City, Iowa

[10] - in Dallas, Texas

[11] - at Conseco Fieldhouse in Indianapolis, Ind.

[12] - at Madison Square Garden in New York, N.Y.

[13] - Coca-Cola Classic in East Lansing, Mich.

[14] - Spartan Great Lakes Classic in Auburn Hills, Mich.

[15] - The Basketbowl at Ford Field in Detroit, Mich.

[16] - Preseason NIT

[17] - at Sun Bowl Classic in El Paso, Texas

[18] - at EA Sports Maui Invitational in Maui, Hawaii

[19] - at Nationwide Arena in Columbus, Ohio

[20] - Comcast Lobo Invitational at The Pit in Albuquerque, N.M.

[21] - Great Alaska Shootout in Anchorage, Alaska

[22] - Boilermaker BlockBuster at Conseco Fieldhouse in Indianapolis, Ind.

[23] - Boilermaker Invitational inWest Lafayette, Ind.

[24] - Rock and Roll Shootout at Gund Arena in Cleveland, Ohio

The Bill Self era of Illinois Basketball was completed following the 2003 season. With three freshmen, one sophomore and just one senior in the starting lineup for the entire season, Self led his young squad to 25 wins, the school's first Big Ten Tournament championship and a victory in the NCAA Tournament. The 78 victories during Self's three years at Illinois are the most wins in a three-year period in school history.

For the second time in three seasons, Illinois featured the Big Ten Player of the Year. Senior Brian Cook earned the award in 2003 after leading the league in scoring at 20 points per game and finishing third in the league in rebounding. Two Illini freshmen, Dee Brown and James Augustine, earned Big Ten All-Freshman Team honors, while classmate Deron Williams joined Brown on a 20-man national all-freshman squad. Sophomore Roger Powell was named to the All-Big Ten Tournament squad after an outstanding run to the title.

Brian Cook

WINS!!

Illini on his shoulders and provided one of the most inspiring performances in Illini history. He scored 26 of his 30 points in the second half, and 19 in the final nine minutes to carry the Illini to a 67-60 win.

In one of the most impressive home victories in some time, Illinois defeated Michigan State, 70-40, in February, holding the Spartans scoreless for a 10-minute stretch in the second half.

A four-game winning streak that started with the win over MSU took the Illini into a conference-title showdown at Wisconsin on March 5 with the winner taking the Big Ten title. In a tightly played game, the Badgers pulled out a 60-59 win on a free throw with four-tenths of a second remaining in the game.

Illinois began the Big Ten Tournament as the No. 2 seed and swept past Northwestern, Indiana and Ohio State to claim its first title in the six-year history of the tournament.

After beginning the season ranked No. 25 in the *USA Today*/ESPN Coaches' Poll, the Illini completed non-conference play with a 10-1 record, including impressive wins over 12th-ranked North Carolina (92-65) and No. 11 Missouri (85-70).

The Illini began Big Ten play on the road at dangerous Minnesota and used 25 points by Cook and 22 from fellow senior Sean Harrington in posting a 76-70 win.

Michigan entered the Jan. 29 game at Champaign undefeated and in first place in the league. The Wolverines jumped out to a 47-39 lead with 9:07 remaining. At that point, Brian Cook loaded the

Illinois entered the NCAA Tournament as a No. 4 seed and defeated Western Kentucky in the first round. A tough 68-60 loss to Notre Dame ended the season for the Illini.

Illinois' 25 victories for the season were the fifth most in school history. Brian Cook and Dee Brown earned All-Big Ten honors for the season, with Cook a unanimous choice for the first team and Brown to the second team.

Seniors Cook and Harrington played in 100 victories during their four-year career, the most victories in a four-year period in school history. Illinois also compiled a 51-2 home record over the past four years, the best mark in the nation for that period.

2002-03 FIGHTING ILLINI HONORS

James Augustine, Fr.
- Big Ten All-Freshman Team

Dee Brown, Fr.
- Second-Team All-Big Ten (Media)
- Third-Team All-Big Ten (Coaches)
- Big Ten All-Freshman Team
- CollegeInsider.com All-Freshman Team
- Big Ten Player of the Week (12/23)
- CBS Player of the Game vs. Indiana (1/18)
- CBS Player of the Game vs. Michigan State (2/2)
- CBS Player of the Game vs. Minnesota (3/9)
- CBS Player of the Game vs. Western Kentucky (3/20)

Brian Cook, Sr.
- Big Ten Player of the Year (Media and Coaches)

- Unanimous First-Team All-Big Ten (Media and Coaches)
- Big Ten Tournament Most Outstanding Player
- Big Ten All-Tournament Team
- Wooden Award Finalist (1 of 22)
- Naismith Award Finalist (1 of 20)
- USBWA National Player of the Year Finalist (1 of 15)
- Senior CLASS Award Finalist (1 of 10)
- CollegeInsider.com All-American and Big Ten Player of the Year
- NABC First-Team All-District 11
- USBWA All-District V
- CBS Player of the Game vs. Indiana (3/15)
- CBS Player of the Game vs. Notre Dame (3/22)
- Big Ten, ESPN.com, *The Sporting News*, FoxSports.com, *College*

Basketball News & Dick Vitale Player of the Week (1/13)
- Big Ten Co-Player of the Week (12/9)
- Preseason Big Ten Player of the Year

Sean Harrington, Sr.
- ESPN2 Player of the Game vs. North Carolina (12/3)

Roger Powell, So.
- Big Ten All-Tournament Team
- CBS Player of the Game vs. Ohio State (2/9)
- CBS Player of the Game vs. Northwestern (2/22)
- CBS Player of the Game vs. Ohio State (3/16)

Deron Williams, Fr.
- CollegeInsider.com All-Freshman Team

Bill Self, Head Coach
- Naismith National Coach of the Year Finalist

2002-03 ALL-BIG TEN TEAMS

AS SELECTED BY COACHES

Player of the Year
Brian Cook, Illinois

Freshman of the Year
Daniel Horton, Michigan

Defensive Player of the Year
Kenneth Lowe, Purdue

First Team
LaVell Blanchard, Michigan
Brian Cook, Illinois*
Willie Deane, Purdue
Kirk Penney, Wisconsin*
Rick Rickert, Minnesota

Second Team
Brent Darby, Ohio State
Devin Harris, Wisconsin
Chris Hill, Michigan State
Daniel Horton, Michigan
Jeff Newton, Indiana

Third Team
Dee Brown, Illinois
Kenneth Lowe, Purdue
Bernard Robinson Jr., Michigan
Bracey Wright, Indiana
Jitim Young, Northwestern

Honorable Mention
Chris Booker, Pur.; Michael
Bauer, Minn.; Tom Coverdale,
Ind.; Maurice Hargrow, Minn.;
Jerry Holman, Minn.; Chauncey
Leslie, Iowa; Jared Reiner, Iowa;
Glen Worley, Iowa.

All-Freshman Team
Dee Brown, Illinois
James Augustine, Illinois
Daniel Horton, Michigan
Alando Tucker, Wisconsin
Bracey Wright, Indiana

AS SELECTED BY MEDIA

Player of the Year
Brian Cook, Illinois

Freshman of the Year
Daniel Horton, Michigan

Coach of the Year
Bo Ryan, Wisconsin

First Team
LaVell Blanchard, Michigan
Brian Cook, Illinois*
Willie Deane, Purdue
Jeff Newton, Indiana
Kirk Penney, Wisconsin*

Second Team
Dee Brown, Illinois
Brent Darby, Ohio State
Chris Hill, Michigan State
Daniel Horton, Michigan
Rick Rickert, Minnesota

Third Team
Devin Harris, Wisconsin
Chauncey Leslie, Iowa
Kenneth Lowe, Purdue
Bernard Robinson Jr., Michigan
Bracey Wright, Indiana

Honorable Mention
Alan Anderson, MSU; Michael
Bauer, Minn.; Sharif Chambliss,
PSU; Tom Coverdale, Ind.; Jeff
Horner, Iowa; Jared Reiner,
Iowa; Alando Tucker, Wisc.;
Brandon Watkins, PSU; Jitim
Young, Northwestern.

*Unanimous

DATE	OPPONENT	W/L, SCORE	ATTENDANCE	HIGH POINTS	HIGH REBOUNDS
11-24-02	LEHIGH	W, 90-56	11,758	15 - Powell	9 - Augustine
					9 - Powell
11-27-02	ARKANSAS-PINE BLUFF	W, 96-43	11,733	17 - Powell	9 - Augustine
12-1-02	WESTERN ILLINOIS	W, 85-56	14,224	17 - Cook	7 - Powell
12-3-02	NORTH CAROLINA @	W, 92-65	16,500	22 - Cook	8 - Cook
12-7-02	vs. Arkansas (at Little Rock, Ark.)	W, 62-58	9,756	18 - Cook	6 - Augustine
12-10-02	EASTERN ILLINOIS	W, 80-68	13,828	25 - Brown	6 - Cook
12-14-02	vs. Temple (at Chicago)	W, 70-54	13,361	25 - Cook	11 - Cook
12-21-02	vs. Missouri (at St. Louis, Mo.)	W, 85-70	22,153	21 - Brown	9 - Cook
12-28-02	at Memphis	L, 74-77	19,268	21 - Cook	9 - Cook
12-30-02	COPPIN STATE	W, 63-37	13,923	20 - Cook	8 - Cook
1-4-03	OAKLAND	W, 88-53	14,837	22 - Cook	11 - Cook
1-7-03	at Minnesota	W, 76-70	13,548	25 - Cook	11 - Cook
1-11-03	WISCONSIN	W, 69-63	16,500	31- Cook	9 - Cook
1-15-03	at Iowa	L, 61-68	15,232	20 - Cook	12 - Cook
1-18-03	at Indiana	L, 66-74	17,456	18 - Brown	7 - Cook
1-22-03	PURDUE	W, 75-62	16,500	22 - Cook	7 - Williams
1-25-03	at Penn State	W, 75-63	9,601	19 - Augustine	12 - Augustine
1-29-03	MICHIGAN	W, 67-60	16,500	30 - Cook	10 - Augustine
2-2-03 at	Michigan State	L, 65-58	14,759	13 - Cook	5 - Cook
					5 - Smith
					5 - Augustine
2-9-03	OHIO STATE	W, 76-57	16,500	22 - Cook	9 - Augustine
2-15-03	at Purdue	L, 61-70	14,123	20 - Cook	7 - Williams
2-18-03	MICHIGAN STATE	W, 70-40	16,500	24 - Brown	8 - Augustine
2-22-03	NORTHWESTERN(at Chicago)	W, 73-61	15,429	20 - Powell	10 - Cook
2-25-03	INDIANA	W, 80-54	16,500	22 - Powell	7 - Cook
					7 - Powell
3-1-03	at Michigan	W, 82-79	13,057	26 - Cook	7 - Cook
					7 - Powell
3-5-03	at Wisconsin	L, 59-60	17,142	25 - Cook	6 - Cook
3-9-03	MINNESOTA	W, 84-60	16,500	22 - Cook	8 - Cook
3-14-03	vs. Northwestern %	W, 94-65	18,895	20 - Cook	12 - Cook
3-15-03	vs. Indiana %	W, 73-72	20,248	25 - Cook	5 - Head
					5 - Smith
3-16-03	vs. Ohio State %	W, 72-59	17,007	16 - Powell	10 - Augustine
3-20-03	vs. Western Kentucky #	W, 65-60	21,250	17 - Cook	10 - Cook
3-22-03	vs. Notre Dame #	W, 68-60	25,767	19 - Cook	16 - Cook

@ = ACC/Big Ten Challenge   % = Big Ten Tournament (at Chicago)   # = NCAA Tournament

	OVERALL	HOME	AWAY	NEUTRAL
Record:	25-7	14-0	3-6	8-1
Big Ten:	11-5	7-0	3-5	1-0
Non-Conference:	14-2	7-0	0-1	7-1

BIG TEN INDIVIDUAL SCORING LEADERS (ALL GAMES)

Player-Team	G	FG	3FG	FT	Pts	Avg
1. Brian Cook-ILL	30	202	27	168	599	20.0
2. Brent Darby-OSU	32	163	55	205	586	18.3
3. Willie Deane-PUR	30	164	48	158	534	17.8
4. Kirk Penney-WIS	32	183	62	91	519	16.2
5. Bracey Wright-IND	30	157	66	106	486	16.2
6. LaVell Blanchard-MICH	30	157	66	105	485	16.2
7. Chauncey Leslie-IOWA	31	179	25	107	490	15.8
8. Rick Rickert-MINN	32	184	41	90	499	15.6
9. Daniel Horton-MICH	30	151	74	81	457	15.2
10. Jeff Newton-IND	34	171	11	154	507	14.9

ILLINOIS INDIVIDUAL STATISTICS (ALL GAMES)

Player	G-GS	Min.-Avg.	FG-FGA/Pct.	3P-3PA/Pct.	FT-FTA/Pct.	OR-DR —	Tot./Avg.	PF-FO	A	TO	BLK	ST	PTS-Avg.
Cook	30-30	940-31.3	202-422/.479	27-89/.303	168-205/.820	44-183 —	227/7.6	88-2	60	83	13	20	599-20.0
Brown	32-31	1090-34.1	142-327/.434	51-155/.329	49-72/.681	35-84 —	119/3.7	56-0	159	62	0	57	384-12.0
Powell	30-19	558-18.6	104-176/.591	20-49/.408	33-57/.579	40-61 —	101/3.4	46-0	12	24	12	9	261-8.7
Head	25-8	509-20.4	68-131/.519	28-66/.424	34-46/.739	23-48 —	71/2.8	42-1	42	40	3	27	198-7.9
Harrington	32-6	718-22.4	76-171/.444	64-144/.444	19-30/.633	2-71 —	73/2.3	63-1	65	25	0	29	235-7.3
Augustine	32-29	697-21.8	94-162/.580	5-14/.357	32-45/.711	64-122—	186/5.8	105-5	25	45	27	20	225-7.0
Williams	32-30	868-27.1	75-176/.426	28-79/.354	24-45/.533	15-80 —	95/3.0	76-2	145	59	5	46	202-6.3
Smith	31-5	539-17.4	60-121/.496	5-11/.455	38-44/.864	23-69 —	92/3.0	64-2	26	42	38	11	163-5.3
Spears	6-0	55-9.2	8-12/.667	0-0/.000	3-7/.429	4-5 —	9/1.5	8-0	6	5	1	1	19-3.2
Wilson	18-0	118-6.6	14-37/.378	4-16/.250	14-18/.778	13-16 —	29/1.6	23-0	8	5	1	4	46-2.6
Ferguson	24-1	218-9.1	11-33/.333	0-3/.000	18-26/.692	11-21 —	32/1.3	19-0	20	20	0	3	40-1.7
Howard	14-1	52-3.7	4-16/.250	1-6/.167	0-0/.000	0-3 —	3/0.2	5-0	7	2	0	0	9-0.6
Huge	8-0	17-2.1	0-3/.000	0-3/.000	4-4/1.000	0-1 —	1/0.1	2-0	0	1	0	0	4-0.5
Thomas	9-0	21-2.3	1-6/.167	0-1/.000	1-4/.250	1-3 —	4/0.4	1-0	0	2	0	0	3-0.3
TEAM						42-49 —	91/2.8			3			
Illinois	32		859-1793/.479	233-636/.366	437-603/.725	317-816—	1133/35.4	598-13	575	418	100	227	2388-74.6
Opponents	32		657-1741/.377	192-621/.309	464-655/.708	356-686—	1042/32.6	576	353	469	84	182	1970-61.6

Score by Periods	1st	2nd	OT	Total
ILLINOIS	1178	1210	0	2388
Opponents	941	1029	0	1970

ILLINOIS TEAM HIGHS AND LOWS

	HIGHS	LOWS
Points	96 vs. Ark-Pine Bluff, 11/27/02	59 vs. Wisconsin, 3/5/03
Field Goals Made	37, 3 times, last vs. Oakland, 1/4/03	22, six times, last vs. Indiana, 3/15/03
Field Goals Attempted	75 vs. Ark-Pine Bluff, 11/27/02	43 vs. Coppin State, 12/30/02
Field Goal Percentage	.617 (37-60) vs. Western Illinois, 12/1/02	.358 (19-53) vs. Michigan, 1/29/03
Three-Point Field Goals Made	12 vs. Ohio State, 2/9/03	3 vs. Northwestern, 2/22/03
Three-Point Field Goals Attempted	31 vs. Memphis, 12/28/02	9 vs. Wisconsin, 3/5/03
Three-Point Field Goal Percentage	.556 vs. Coppin State, 12/30/02	.211 (4-19) vs. Iowa, 1/15/03
Free Throws Made	26 vs. Northwestern, 3/14/03	4 vs. Western Illinois, 12/1/02
Free Throws Attempted	34 vs. Northwestern, 3/14/03	5 vs. Western Illinois, 12/1/02
Free Throw Percentage	.905 (19-21) vs. Temple, 12/14/02	.400 (8-20) vs. Eastern Illinois, 12/10/02
Rebounds	50 vs. Ark-Pine Bluff, 11/27/02	21 vs. Arkansas, 12/7/02
Assists	26 vs. Minnesota, 3/9/03	12, Wisconsin, 3/5/03
Turnovers	20 vs. Ohio State, 2/9/03	5 vs. Indiana, 2/25/03
Blocks	8 vs. Memphis, 12/28/02 and Oakland, 1/4/03	0, four times, last vs. Michigan St., 2/2/03
Steals	13 vs. Michigan State, 2/18/03	2 vs. Indiana, 1/18/03
Fouls	27 vs. Purdue, 1/22/03	12 vs. Ark-Pine Bluff, 11/27/02

OPPONENT TEAM HIGHS AND LOWS

	HIGHS	LOWS
Points	79, Michigan, 3/1/03	37, Coppin State, 12/30/02
Field Goals Made	27, Michigan, 3/1/03	12, Coppin State, 12/30/02
Field Goals Attempted	68, Minnesota, 3/9/03	41, Coppin State, 12/30/02
Field Goal Percentage	.482, Michigan, 3/1/03	.288 (17-59), Temple, 12/14/02
Three-Point Field Goals Made	11, Michigan, 3/1/03	2, Coppin State, 12/30/02 and Iowa, 1/15/03
Three-Point Field Goals Attempted	28, Temple, 12/14/02	8, Coppin State, 12/30/02
Three-Point Field Goal Percentage	.500 (8-16), Indiana, 3/15/03	.167 (2-12), Iowa, 1/15/03
Free Throws Made	29, Minnesota, 1/7/03 and Purdue, 2/15/03	3, Michigan State, 2/18/03
Free Throws Attempted	36, Purdue, 2/15/03	8, Michigan State, 2/18/03
Free Throw Percentage	.957 (22-23), Northwestern, 3/14/03	.316 (6-19), Oakland, 1/4/03
Rebounds	47, Indiana, 1/18/03	20, Ark-Pine Bluff, 11/27/02
Assists	18, Memphis, 12/28/02	6, Michigan State, 2/18/03
Turnovers	23, Ark-Pine Bluff, 11/27/02	5, Indiana, 1/18/03
Blocks	8, Indiana, 1/18/03	0, four times, last Wisconsin, 1/11/03
Steals	12, Temple, 12/14/02 and Michigan St., 2/2/03	0, Indiana, 2/25/03
Fouls	23, three times, last Indiana, 3/15/03	11, Western Illinois, 12/1/02

ILLINOIS AND OPPONENT INDIVIDUAL HIGHS

	ILLINOIS	OPPONENT
Points	31, Brian Cook vs. Wisconsin, 1/11/03	30, Henry Domercant, Eastern Illinois, 12/10/02
Field Goals	12, Brian Cook vs. Wisconsin, 1/11/03	10, Henry Domercant, Eastern Illinois, 12/10/02
Field Goal Attempts	19, Brian Cook, three times, last vs. Indiana, 2/25/03	23, Brent Darby, Ohio State, 3/16/03
Field Goal Percentage (min. 7 att.)	.818 (9-11), Brian Cook vs. Oakland, 1/4/03	.750 (6-8), Jesse Mackinson, Eastern Illinois, 12/10/02
		.750 (6-8), Jason Burke, Northwestern, 2/22/03
Three-Point Field Goals Made	6, Sean Harrington vs. North Carolina, 12/3/02	7, LaVell Blanchard, Michigan, 3/1/03
	6, Sean Harrington vs. Coppin State, 12/30/02	
	6, Sean Harrington vs. Minnesota, 1/7/03	
Three-Point Field Goal Attempts	11, Dee Brown vs. Memphis, 12/28/02	14, Sharif Chambliss, Penn State, 1/25/03
Three-Point Field Goal Pct. (min. 5 att.)	.800 (4-5), Sean Harrington vs. Ohio State, 3/16/03	.667 (4-6), Anthony Rice, Memphis, 12/28/02
		.667 (4-6), Sean Connolly, Ohio State, 3/16/03
Free Throws Made	13 (13-17), Brian Cook vs. Minnesota, 1/7/03	13, (13-15), Kenneth Lowe, Purdue, 2/15/03
Free Throws Attempted	17 (13-17), Brian Cook vs. Minnesota, 1/7/03	15, (13-15), Kenneth Lowe, Purdue, 2/15/03
Free Throw Percentage (min. 8 att.)	1.000 (8-8), Brian Cook vs. Memphis, 12/28/02	1.000 (10-10), Maurice Hargrow, Minnesota, 1/7/03
	1.000 (10-10), Brian Cook, vs. Missouri, 12/21/02	1.000 (9-9), Davor Duvancic, N'western, 3/14/03
Rebounds	12, Brian Cook vs. Iowa, 1/15/03	12, Chris Massie, Memphis, 12/28/02
	12, James Augustine vs. Penn State, 1/25/03	12, Kirk Penney, Wisconsin, 1/11/03
Assists	11, Dee Brown vs. Penn State, 1/25/03	6, Brandon Watkins, Penn State, 1/25/03
		6, Bernard Robinson Jr., Michigan, 3/1/03
		6, Brent Darby, Ohio State, 3/16/03
Steals	5, Sean Harrington vs. North Carolina, 12/3/02	5, Rawle Marshall, Oakland, 1/4/03
	5, Dee Brown vs. Michigan State, 2/18/03	5, Paul Davis, Michigan St., 2/2/03
	5, Dee Brown vs. Northwestern, 2/22/03	
Blocks	5, James Augustine vs. Oakland, 1/4/03	5, Jeff Newton, Indiana, 1/18/03
	5, Nick Smith vs. Minnesota, 3/9/03	

FIELD GOAL PCT.

(Min. 3.0 made per game)

Player-Team	G	FG	FGA	Pct
1. Holman, Jerry-MINN	33	138	233	.592
2. Powell, Roger-ILL	30	104	176	.591
3. Reiner, Jared-IOWA	28	92	170	.541
4. Tucker, Alando-WIS	32	139	261	.533
5. Sonderleiter, Sean-IOWA	28	90	174	.517
6. Radinovic, Velimir-OSU	30	95	185	.514
7. Leslie, Chauncey-IOWA	31	179	364	.492
8. Young, Jitim-NU	29	140	288	.486
9. Abram, Lester-MICH	30	104	217	.479
10. Cook, Brian-ILL	30	202	422	.479

3-POINT FG PCT.

(Min 1.5 made per game)

Player-Team	G	3FG	FGA	Pct
1. Harrington, Sean-ILL	32	64	144	.444
2. Blanchard, LaVell-MICH	30	66	158	.418
3. Connolly, Sean-OSU	30	66	162	.407
4. Hill, Chris-MSU	35	95	235	.404
5. Riley, DeForrest-PSU	28	46	115	.400
6. Harris, Devin-WIS	32	53	137	.387
7. Penney, Kirk-WIS	32	62	161	.385
8. Chambliss, Sharif-PSU	28	89	232	.384
9. Hornsby, Kyle-IND	34	54	142	.380
10. Wright, Bracey-IND	30	66	176	.375

FREE THROW PCT.

(Min. 2.0 made per game)

Player-Team	G	FTM	FTA	Pct
1. Chambliss, Sharif-PSU	28	64	71	.901
2. Lowe, Kenneth-PUR	27	126	142	.887
3. Abram, Lester-MICH	30	89	104	.856
4. Robinson, Bernard-MICH	29	78	92	.848
5. Anderson, Alan-MSU	32	128	152	.842
6. Coverdale, Tom-IND	34	92	112	.821
7. Owens, Freddie-WIS	32	73	89	.820
8. Cook, Brian-ILL	30	168	205	.820
9. Blanchard, LaVell-MICH	30	105	129	.814
10. Darby, Brent-OSU	32	205	253	.810

ASSISTS

Player-Team	G	Assists	Avg
1. Brown, Dee-ILL	32	159	4.97
2. Burleson, Kevin-MINN	33	160	4.85
3. Williams, Deron-ILL	32	145	4.53
4. Horner, Jeff-IOWA	31	140	4.52
5. Coverdale, Tom-IND	34	152	4.47
6. Horton, Daniel-MICH	30	134	4.47
7. Darby, Brent-OSU	32	141	4.41
8. Watkins, Brandon-PSU	28	103	3.68
9. Hill, Chris-MSU	35	128	3.66
10. Robinson, Bernard-MICH	29	100	3.45

REBOUNDING

Player-Team	G	O-D	Tot	Avg
1. Reiner, Jared-IOWA	28	74-157	231	8.2
2. Newton, Jeff-IND	34	74-206	280	8.2
3. Cook, Brian-ILL	30	44-183	227	7.6
4. Blanchard, LaVell-MICH	30	56-149	205	6.8
5. Wilkinson, Mike-WIS	32	74-142	216	6.8
5. Jagla, Jan-PSU	28	55-134	189	6.8
7. Rickert, Rick-MICH	32	58-140	198	6.2
8. Robinson, Bernard-MICH	29	44-134	178	6.1
9. Radinovic, Velimir-OSU	30	72-111	183	6.1
10. Jenkins, Shun-OSU	24	55-91	146	6.1

STEALS

Player-Team	G	Steals	Avg
1. Harris, Devin-WIS	32	65	2.03
2. Darby, Brent-OSU	32	58	1.81
3. Brown, Dee-ILL	32	57	1.78
4. Deane, Willie-PUR	30	52	1.73
5. Burleson, Kevin-MINN	33	55	1.67
6. Young, Jitim-NU	29	47	1.62
7. Hill, Chris-MSU	35	51	1.46
8. Leslie, Chauncey-IOWA	31	45	1.45
9. Williams, Deron-ILL	32	46	1.44
10. Parker, T.J.-NU	29	40	1.38

BLOCKED SHOTS

Player-Team	G	Blocks	Avg
1. Leach, George-IND	32	79	2.47
2. Bauer, Michael-MINN	33	54	1.64
3. Jagla, Jan-PSU	28	45	1.61
4. Holman, Jerry-MINN	33	52	1.58
5. Newton, Jeff-IND	34	52	1.53
6. Jennings, Aaron-NU	29	36	1.24
7. Smith, Nick-ILL	31	38	1.23
8. Reiner, Jared-IOWA	28	34	1.21
9. Hunter, Chris-MICH	30	35	1.17
10. Worley, Glen-IOWA	31	34	1.10

3-PT FIELD GOALS PER GAME

Player-Team	G	3FG	Avg.
1. Chambliss, Sharif-PSU	28	89	3.18
2. Hill, Chris-MSU	35	95	2.71
3. Horton, Daniel-MICH	30	74	2.47
4. Coverdale, Tom-IND	34	75	2.21
5. Connolly, Sean-OSU	30	66	2.20
5. Wright, Bracey-IND	30	66	2.20
5. Blanchard, LaVell-MICH	30	66	2.20
8. Bauer, Michael-MINN	33	71	2.15
9. Harrington, Sean-ILL	32	64	2.00
10. Penney, Kirk-WIS	32	62	1.94

ASST/TURNOVER RATIO

Player-Team	G	A	Avg	TO	Avg	Ratio
1. Brown, Dee-ILL	32	159	5.0	62	1.9	2.56
2. Williams, Deron-ILL	32	145	4.5	59	1.8	2.46
3. Coverdale, Tom-IND	34	152	4.5	64	1.9	2.38
4. Harris, Devin-WIS	32	98	3.1	51	1.6	1.92
5. Burleson, Kevin-MINN	33	160	4.8	84	2.5	1.90
6. Horner, Jeff-IOWA	31	140	4.5	77	2.5	1.82
7. Hill, Chris-MSU	35	128	3.7	86	2.5	1.49
8. Anderson, Alan-MSU	32	104	3.2	80	2.5	1.30
9. Penney, Kirk-WIS	32	100	3.1	80	2.5	1.25
10. Horton, Daniel-MICH	30	134	4.5	110	3.7	1.22

Richard Keene, 29, played for the Illini from 1992-96. The shooting guard from Collinsville, Ill., ranks 27th on the all-time scoring list at 9.4 points per game and is second in career three-pointers made behind Cory Bradford. These days Rich lives and works in the St. Louis area, where he and his wife, Sara, are raising two new Illini fans.

What are you doing these days?

RK: I work in sales for LaBarge Pipe & Steel, one of the largest carbon steel pipe distributors to oil and gas companies. I've been here about a year and a half. Before that I was in radio sales for about a year. And before that I was bouncing around playing ball. I played in the CBA in Ft. Wayne, Ind., and then had a short stint over in Dubai [Tunisia]. I went back to school and finished my degree in sports management in 2000 after bad knees forced me out of the game. The older you get, the harder it is to stay in shape. So, I just hung it up. Once you go to another country you realize how good we have it here in the States.

Have you started a family?

RK: Yes, I got married two years ago. My wife, Sara, and I have a 16-month-old son, RJ, and another one, a girl, on the way in February. We're going to name her Sophia.

What's your greatest memory of your time spent at UI?

RK: All the Mizzou games were great. The triple overtime game [on Dec. 22, 1993] was awesome. Great environment. Great atmosphere. And then, my freshman year when Kaufmann beat Iowa with the shot. That was unbelievable. Then playing in postseason was awesome. We lost to Vandy in the second round after beating them by 40 earlier. The next year we lost to Georgetown in Tulsa. Then, the next was to Tulsa in Albany, N.Y.

Which of your former teammates do you stay in touch with?

RK: I still talk to [Chris] Gandy, Tommy Michael, and TJ [Wheeler]. Every couple of weeks we talk.

What do you miss most about Champaign-Urbana?

RK: Everything. The college life is something you don't appreciate until it's gone—just hanging out with friends. I watch games on TV every chance I get. Got to deal with Mizzou people, but the U of I's still strong here. I try to hit a game or two a year.

That reunion that Self set up was cool last year that Self set up. That 100th year reunion next year sounds great!

Who's your favorite current Illini?

RK: I like Dee—the way he runs the team. He seems like a great player to play with. He looks for his shot but is always looking to get his teammates involved too.

Do you know Coach Weber?

RK: I saw him at a St. Louis Cardinal game and said "Hi" to him. He recognized me. We roughed up his teams a couple of times (while Weber was at Purdue). My dad played at SIU so I'm definitely familiar with him there. I also had a lot of friends that went down there. I think he'll do a good job.